Don't Just Do Something, Sit There

CHANDOS
INFORMATION PROFESSIONAL SERIES

Series Editor: Ruth Rikowski
(email: Rikowskigr@aol.com)

Chandos' new series of books is aimed at the busy information professional. They have been specially commissioned to provide the reader with an authoritative view of current thinking. They are designed to provide easy-to-read and (most importantly) practical coverage of topics that are of interest to librarians and other information professionals. If you would like a full listing of current and forthcoming titles, please visit www.chandospublishing.com or email wp@woodheadpublishing.com or telephone +44 (0) 1223 499140.

New authors: we are always pleased to receive ideas for new titles; if you would like to write a book for Chandos, please contact Dr Glyn Jones on email gjones@chandospublishing.com or telephone number +44 (0) 1993 848726.

Bulk orders: some organisations buy a number of copies of our books. If you are interested in doing this, we would be pleased to discuss a discount. Please email wp@woodheadpublishing.com or telephone +44 (0) 1223 499140.

Don't Just Do Something, Sit There

An introduction to non-directive coaching

BOB THOMSON

CHANDOS
PUBLISHING

Oxford Cambridge New Delhi

Chandos Publishing
Hexagon House
Avenue 4
Station Lane
Witney
Oxford OX28 4BN
UK
Tel: +44 (0) 1993 848726
Email: info@chandospublishing.com
www.chandospublishing.com

Chandos Publishing is an imprint of Woodhead Publishing Limited

Woodhead Publishing Limited
80 High Street
Sawston
Cambridge CB22 3HJ
UK
Tel: +44 (0) 1223 499140
Fax: +44 (0) 1223 832819
www.woodheadpublishing.com

First published in 2009

ISBN: 978-1-84334-429-2 (print)
ISBN: 978-1-78063-206-3 (online)

© R. Thomson, 2009

British Library Cataloguing-in-Publication Data.
A catalogue record for this book is available from the British Library.

Typeset by Domex e-Data Pvt. Ltd.
Printed in the UK and USA.

Printed in the UK by 4edge Limited - www.4edge.co.uk

To the memory of my parents
Josephine Thomson (1927–2004)
and Bobby Thomson (1926–2006)

It is the province of knowledge to speak, and it is the privilege of wisdom to listen.

Oliver Wendell Holmes

Contents

List of figures and tables   *xv*

About the author   *xvii*

Preface   *xix*

1   What is non-directive coaching?   **1**

Introduction   1

Silent coaching   1

Ideas arising from the silent coaching exercise   4

Defining coaching   6

Directive and non-directive behaviours   8

Directive and non-directive approaches   11

Coaching or mentoring?   13

Awareness and responsibility   15

2   Listening   **17**

Introduction   17

Levels of listening   18

Listening with the head, the heart and the gut   22

Silence   25

Active, attentive listening   26

Why listening is so important   27

Listening and being non-directive   28

3   Questioning   **31**

Introduction   31

Listening and questioning   31

	Open and closed questions	33
	Crisp questions	36
	Other types of question	37
	Reframing	38
	Leading questions	39
	Incisive questions	40
	What do you do when you don't know what question to ask?	42
	Questioning and being non-directive	43
4	**Playing back**	**45**
	Introduction	45
	Three ways of playing back to the client	45
	Using the client's exact words	47
	Managing the conversation	47
	Communicating empathic understanding	49
	Taking notes	50
5	**Becoming a capable coach**	**53**
	Introduction	53
	Learning from experience	53
	Coaching trios	55
	Modifying the GROW model	57
	Practice clients	59
	Journalling	61
	Supervision	62
	Coaching qualifications	64
	Going round the learning cycle	65
6	**Directive and non-directive coaching**	**67**
	Introduction	67
	The directive to non-directive spectrum	68

Giving advice, making suggestions and offering
feedback   69

The skilled helper   72

Advice on giving advice   73

Providing information   75

Advice and solutions from a line manager   76

Coaching versus mentoring   78

Are awareness and responsibility enough?   79

Some evidence   80

7   **Ethical and other issues in coaching**   **83**

Introduction   83

The EMCC code of ethics   83

A code of ethics   84

Two-way contracting   86

Three-way contracting: who is the client?   87

Evaluation   90

Keeping notes and records   91

Supervision   94

8   **Tools you might use in coaching**   **95**

Introduction   95

Rich pictures   95

Sorting cards   98

Writing a letter   100

The empty chair   101

Psychometric tools   102

360-degree feedback   104

9   **Coaching as a line manager**   **109**

Introduction   109

Similarities   109

Differences 110

The coaching dance 112

Coaching in the hurly burly 114

Coaching a team 118

A coaching culture 119

Servant-leadership 120

10 Metaphor and clean language **125**

Introduction 125

Metaphor 125

Clean language and symbolic modelling 129

Using metaphor and clean language in coaching 133

11 Psychological bases of coaching **137**

Introduction 137

The three schools of Western psychology 137

Transactional analysis 139

Psychosynthesis 144

A community of selves 146

Applying these ideas in coaching 148

12 The foundations of a non-directive approach **151**

Introduction 151

Carl Rogers and the person-centred approach 151

Carl Rogers' three conditions for effective facilitation 153

Tim Gallwey and the inner game 154

Two equations 158

Rogers and Gallwey 159

13 The inner game of coaching **161**

Introduction 161

Preparing for a coaching session 162

Interference during a coaching session 164

Potential and Self Two 168

14   Becoming an even more capable coach   **173**

Introduction   173

Some questions for you   173

Some things I am taking from writing the book   174

Some questions for me   175

Bibliography   **177**

Index   **183**

List of figures and tables

Figures

1.1   Directive and non-directive coaching behaviours   10
1.2   Types of coaching   12
2.1   Levels of listening   21
2.2   The iceberg model of listening   23
5.1   The learning cycle   54
5.2   A coaching learning cycle   66
8.1   A picture   96

Tables

3.1   Closed and open questions   35
6.1   Dimensions of directive and non-directive
      coaching   68
8.1   Dimensions of the Myers-Briggs Type Indicator   103
9.1   The coaching dance (after David Hemery)   113

About the author

Bob Thomson has worked in management development since 1988. He is currently a Learning and Development Adviser at the University of Warwick and was previously Leadership Development Manager at National Grid Transco. In his role he coaches individuals, runs the University's Certificate in Coaching, and supervises the Warwick Coaching Scheme, in which members of staff act as coaches to other members of staff.

His previous book, *Growing People: Learning and developing from day to day experience*, was published by Chandos in 2006.

Before moving into management development he worked as an economist for 11 years with British Steel and ICI.

Bob has degrees in Maths, in Economics and in Management Learning. He also has a Certificate in Counselling and a Certificate in Coaching.

He is married with four children and lives in Stratford upon Avon.

The author may be contacted at:

E-mail: *bob.thomson@warwick.ac.uk*

Preface

In writing this book I have had in mind two imaginary readers. The first is someone who wants to learn how to coach and is looking for some ideas to give them the basis for their practice. The second is a reader who is already engaged in coaching and wants to reflect on their practice in order to enhance their effectiveness. I want to offer both kinds of reader ideas to consider in the hope that they will extract what seems meaningful, relevant and useful for their own situation.

There is no single way to coach effectively. I do take the view, however, that it is very useful for a coach to be clear about what they are trying to do when they sit down to engage in a coaching conversation with a client. In particular, I think it is important for a coach to have thought through how directive or non-directive they intend to be with their clients. My own preference is to be primarily non-directive, and this stance significantly shapes the ideas offered in the book. I am, as someone once said to me, directive about the importance of being non-directive. As you read the book, bear in mind my bias and come to your own conclusions about how you wish to work at different points on the directive to non-directive spectrum.

I believe that deep and sustained learning only comes through experience. Experience on its own isn't enough, however. You need to reflect upon and make sense of your experience to create knowledge, and this knowledge deepens when it is applied in practice. I encourage you, therefore, to try out some of the ideas from the book and then reflect upon and make sense of this experience.

The book falls into three parts. The first four chapters offer an introduction to coaching and the basic skills needed to coach well. Chapter 1 sets out the key ideas that underpin coaching, particularly the notion that as a coach you are trying to do two things – to raise *awareness* in the client and to encourage them to take *responsibility* to act. This opening chapter also introduces the widely-used GROW framework for structuring a coaching conversation, explores the difference between coaching and mentoring, and looks at the various behaviours that lie along the spectrum from directive to non-directive coaching. Chapters 2–4 then explore in some detail what I see as the three fundamental skills needed to coach successfully – listening to understand the client, asking open questions to encourage them to think, and playing back what they have communicated.

In Chapters 5–10 we then explore a number of topics that develop these basic themes and look at other ideas that you might use in your work as a coach. Chapter 5 considers the notion of learning from experience and offers some ideas to help you to practise your coaching skills and to reflect systematically upon your practice. Chapter 6 explores a number of ethical and other coaching issues – such as confidentiality – that you need to think through and to work out where you personally stand. In Chapter 7 we look again at the differences between directive and non-directive coaching, inviting you to consider where you operate as a coach on the directive to non-directive spectrum. Chapter 8 looks at a number of practical tools that you might bring into a coaching session, including rich pictures, card sorts, psychometrics and 360-degree feedback.

The focus in Chapter 9 is on how a line manager within an organisation can use coaching as a key aspect of the way in which they manage other people. In Chapter 10 we explore two ideas – metaphor and clean language – that you might use or adapt in your coaching practice.

The closing chapters take a more philosophical perspective on coaching. Chapter 11 looks briefly at the three main schools of psychology – psychoanalytic, cognitive-behavioural and humanistic – and considers how you might adapt some of the ideas from these different approaches in your own practice as a coach. Chapter 12 summarises the ideas of Carl Rogers and Tim Gallwey, which, for me, provide the philosophical foundations for a primarily non-directive approach to coaching. Chapter 13 develops Gallwey's idea of the inner game, exploring the inner game that takes place in the mind of the coach as they converse with their client. The brief final chapter invites you to summarise what you are taking from the book and offers a few reflections of my own.

I first came across the phrase that is the title of the book in 1983 when I began a Certificate in Counselling at the University of Manchester. One of the tutors, George Henshaw, a wise and experienced counsellor, offered us a motto for the course: *Don't Just Do Something, Sit There.*

There are a number of people and experiences that have helped me in my own development as a coach and which have shaped the ideas explored in the book. In 1998 I was privileged to take part in the first coaching programme offered by the School of Coaching, facilitated by Myles Downey and Jane Meyler. I owe a particular debt to Myles Downey, many of whose views are reflected in the text of the book.

While working at Transco and later at National Grid Transco, I commissioned programmes to help managers to develop their coaching skills. I had the good fortune to work on these programmes alongside some great coaches, such as

John Whitmore, David Hemery, David Whitaker, Sue Slocombe and Charles Brook.

You will see in the various quotes throughout the book that I am indebted to a number of other people whose writings have influenced my approach to coaching – notably Carl Rogers, Tim Gallwey, Alison Hardingham and Nancy Kline. I have also benefited over the years from simulating conversation with coaches and management development consultants such as Elspeth May, Sue Godfrey, Robin Linnecar, Nick Cowley, Jenny Summerfield, Vicki Espin, Steve Schneider, Madeline McGill, Andrew Munro and Gina Hayden.

My views on coaching have also been shaped by my experience working with clients, and I would like to thank all of them for allowing me the privilege of listening to them as they worked through their issues. I am also grateful to Richard Worsley for his very supportive supervision of my practice as a coach.

Thank you too to the various participants on the Certificate in Coaching at the University of Warwick with whom I have explored the ideas set out in the book. Their views and feedback have been very helpful in sharpening my thinking. A special thanks to Cathie Zara who set up the Certificate and invited me to facilitate it, and to Fiona Kaplan with whom I have worked on the programme.

Thanks also to a number of past and present colleagues who have commented on drafts of the book and whose company I have hugely valued, including Jim Borritt, Sean Murphy, Thea Mills, Gill de Calvo, Manus Conaghan, Eve Uhlig, Anne Wilson, Lesley Young and Philip Harris-Worthington.

Thank you to Dr Glyn Jones of Chandos Publishing (Oxford) Ltd who has again been straightforward to collaborate with, and to Neill Johnstone for transforming my text into the final product.

I'd like to thank my wife, Val, and our children, David, Eleanor, Dominic and Olivia for their love and support. Each of them knows that I'm sometimes better at the theory rather than the practice of listening non-judgmentally – particularly when I have a strong attachment to the outcome!

Finally, I dedicate the book with love and gratitude to the memory of my Mum and Dad, Josephine and Bobby Thomson.

What is non-directive coaching?

Introduction

In this opening chapter I'd like to set out some key ideas that underpin coaching, particularly the notion that as a coach you are trying to do two things – to raise *awareness* in the client and to encourage them to take *responsibility* to act. We will also look at the spectrum of directive to non-directive coaching, consider the difference between coaching and mentoring, and offer definitions of coaching and mentoring. The chapter also sets out the widely-used GROW framework for structuring a coaching conversation.

Silent coaching

I will introduce the notion of non-directive coaching by inviting you to do an exercise that I use regularly at the start of programmes to develop coaching skills. I have to admit that when I am reading a book, I generally don't stop to complete an exercise, preferring instead to move on and make sense of what is being offered. Nevertheless, I encourage you to try this before reading on. It will take you around 20 minutes, and you will need a few sheets of paper and a pen or pencil.

To do the exercise you need to have in mind an issue facing you that you would genuinely like to spend 20 minutes thinking about. The issue has to be a real one, not an imaginary situation. It may be work-related or it could be a personal issue that has nothing to do with work. It has to be current in the sense that you are not sure how to proceed – not an issue that you resolved last year or one that you might hypothetically face in the future. It also needs to be something that actually matters to you. I suggest you don't use an issue that you've been wrestling with for years and years. Finally, it needs to be an issue where you are reasonably central to the action – not a problem that belongs to a friend of yours.

I am going to pose 20 questions to structure your thinking about the issue. Simply write down your answer to each question as we go through them. We will look at the structure behind the questions later.

Begin by writing down in a sentence the issue that you want to think about.

Now, here are the 20 questions. Because I don't know what you're writing or how your thinking is progressing, some of my questions may not be relevant to you. If you read a question that doesn't seem appropriate, just move on to the next question. I will also ask you to draw a line across the page at four points – this will help to explain the structure behind the questions later.

- What are you trying to achieve?
- Imagine that you have successfully addressed your issue. What does success look like?
- What does success feel like?
- What do you really, really want?

Draw a line across the page.

- What is going on that makes this an issue for you?
- Who is involved?
- What assumptions are you making?
- What – if anything – have you already done to address the situation?
- And what has been the effect of what you have done so far?

Draw a line across the page.

- What options do you have?
- What else might you do?
- If you had absolutely no constraints – of time or money or power or health – what would you do?
- If you had a really wise friend, what would they do in your shoes?

Draw a line across the page.

Your answers to the last four questions – that is, between the last two lines – have generated a set of options. Some of these options may be quite practical, while others are completely impractical. Looking back at these options, rate them quickly on a scale of 1 to 10 on how practical they seem (where 10 means totally practical). Don't worry about scoring too accurately – we are only really interested in practical options which score 8, 9 or 10, say.

- From your list of options, which options will you actually pursue?
- For each chosen option, what specifically will you do?
- What help or support do you need?
- What deadlines will you set for yourself?
- What is the first step that you will take?

Draw a line across the page.

This is the end of the silent coaching questions. I would like you to answer one more question, which concerns the process you have just been through rather than the content of what you have written.

- What was the effect of these questions?

Ideas arising from the silent coaching exercise

I generally find that most, though not all, participants on a coaching skills programme find the silent coaching exercise powerful. Incidentally, it is called silent coaching because, although the facilitator speaks, the participants are silent as they write down their answers. Thus, while it is an exercise to demonstrate some aspects of coaching, it is not coaching as such, as we shall see later.

The first idea that usually emerges from the exercise is that it is possible to help someone without being an expert in their field. Indeed, the exercise demonstrates that you can help someone without even knowing what their issue is. The exercise is an antidote to the notion that to help someone you need to give them advice or tell them what to do.

I first encountered silent coaching when I worked with John Whitmore and his colleagues from Performance Consultants to help managers in the gas pipeline company, Transco, to develop their coaching skills. The most common difficulty Transco managers had in developing their coaching skills was that they continually stepped in to offer solutions to the person they were coaching. Managers are paid to solve problems, often in a very busy environment, and it seems unusual not to step in with solutions. The theme of this book, however, is that you will generally have much greater, deeper and longer lasting impact if you help others to solve their own problems.

So, the first message from the silent coaching exercise is that you can help someone without telling them what to do. How does this happen? We will explore in some depth how this happens in a coaching relationship, but for the moment simply note that the exercise is built around asking open questions that encourage the client to think. Chapter 3 will consider the art of asking good questions in more detail. One thing that we will see is that the best questions arise out of what the client says. In the silent coaching exercise, the coach does not have this information but nevertheless, asking open questions helps the other to think purposefully about their issue. The second message from the exercise is the power of questioning.

Finally, the exercise introduces a framework to structure a coaching conversation called the GROW model. The questions above – separated by the lines drawn across the page – are structured around four areas:

- Goal: What are you trying to achieve?
- Reality: What is currently going on?
- Options: What could you do?
- Will: What will you do?

The GROW framework, developed originally by Graham Alexander in the 1980s in his work with senior executives, is a very practical framework to structure a conversation to enable another person to think through their situation and come up with a plan of action. I find that people learning to coach initially apply the model somewhat rigidly, using the questions as a crib sheet. There is nothing magical about the precise questions set out in the silent coaching exercise – indeed other questions crafted in response to the client's answers will be more appropriate. In addition, you will find that you will need to work flexibly with the steps in GROW. Sometimes the client's goal will be very clear, and you will not need to spend a lot of time in this stage. On other occasions, you will need to take considerable time to help the client clarify their goal. Again, you will sometimes find that exploration of reality or options leads to the insight that the goal as originally formulated is not achievable and so you need to track back to help the client to revise their goal.

Learning a new skill, such as coaching, is like learning to drive a car. At first, you may mechanically apply a set of instructions, such as the sequence *mirror – signal – manoeuvre*. But with increasing practice comes increasing competence, confidence, and the ability to apply technique flexibly. So, as you experiment with the GROW model, you may wish to stick initially to the above questions and, as your familiarity and ability develop, begin to use the model more flexibly and to create your own open questions. Moreover, just as you would expect your driving skills to improve as you take more lessons, so too your ability to coach well will develop over time with increasing practice and experience.

We will revisit the GROW model in Chapter 5 on becoming a capable coach.

Defining coaching

In my book *Growing People* I offered the following as my preferred definition of coaching:

> Coaching is a relationship to facilitate the performance, learning or development of another. (Thomson, 2006)

This was a variation of a definition I first encountered at the School of Coaching, and offered by Myles Downey in his book, *Effective Coaching*:

> Coaching is the art of facilitating the performance, learning or development of another. (Downey, 2003)

I do not intend to offer a host of definitions, but here is one more that has heavily influenced my thinking. It is taken from John Whitmore's book *Coaching for Performance*:

> Coaching is unlocking a person's potential to maximize their own performance. It is helping them to learn rather than teaching them. (Whitmore, 2002)

I wouldn't disagree with any of these definitions, and would emphasise a number of points.

First, coaching is a relationship between two people (or perhaps between one person and a team). We will look in more detail later at what characterises an effective coaching relationship.

Second, coaching is an art not a science. While the GROW model, for instance, is a useful framework for structuring a coaching conversation, there is no prescription that guarantees that a coaching conversation will be successful. The coach is continually drawing on their experience and their intuition to shape what they do next.

Third, coaching is about facilitating. It is working *with* someone, not doing something *to* them. This is reflected in John Whitmore's point that coaching is about helping someone to learn, not teaching them. This is another notion that we will revisit later.

Having worked with these definitions for a number of years, I want to add something to offer a definition that says a bit more about what is going on in the coaching relationship:

> Coaching occurs through a series of conversations in which one person uses their ability to listen, to ask questions and to play back what they have heard to create a relationship of rapport and trust that enables the other to clarify what matters to them and to work out what to do to achieve their aspirations.

There are a number of new points in this expanded definition. First, coaching is seen as a series of conversations. (Face-to-face coaching might be supplemented by phone calls or e-mails. Indeed, for reasons of logistics or cost, some coaching relationships may be based exclusively on these forms of communication.)

Second, the definition introduces three basic skills that will be explored in the following three chapters – listening, questioning and playing back.

Third, the definition offers a couple of pointers to the nature of an effective coaching relationship – one based on rapport and trust.

Fourth, the definition emphasises that the role of the coach is to help the client to articulate their goals and how they will set about achieving them.

Directive and non-directive behaviours

As you develop your practice as a coach, a fundamental dimension that you need to consider is how directive or non-directive you wish to be. Being clear about your approach will help you continually in choosing what to do next in a coaching session or in managing a coaching relationship.

Here is a list of ten behaviours that you might engage in as a coach. I have simply listed them alphabetically. As an exercise, take a few minutes to rearrange the behaviours along a spectrum from the most directive behaviours at one end to the most non-directive behaviours at the other.

- asking questions that raise awareness;
- giving advice;
- giving feedback;
- instructing;
- listening to understand;
- making suggestions;
- offering guidance;
- paraphrasing;
- reflecting;
- summarising.

I use this exercise, which I first experienced at the School of Coaching, to highlight that as a coach there are a number of behaviours you might engage in, and to introduce this fundamental question of how directive or non-directive you wish to be. My own approach to coaching is to be predominantly non-directive. One of my intentions in this book is to continually invite you, the reader, to consider where you stand in your approach and practice as a coach. I am aware that there is something of a paradox in setting out for others the merits of being non-directive. So, let's note for now that other coaches successfully employ a style which is closer to the directive end of the spectrum, and some managers are very successful using a directive or even autocratic approach.

When you are coaching you will find that you are continually faced with choices about what to do next and how to respond. *What question should I ask now? How do I deal with this silence? The session seems to be going nowhere, so what should I do?* And so on. There are a host of possible responses, and choosing the right response is an art rather than a science. A vital notion to bear in mind when you say or do anything is your intention. When you ask a question, give advice or offer a summary, what is your intention at that point?

Figure 1.1 offers one answer to the task of arranging the behaviours along the directive–non-directive spectrum.

Figure 1.1   Directive and non-directive coaching behaviours

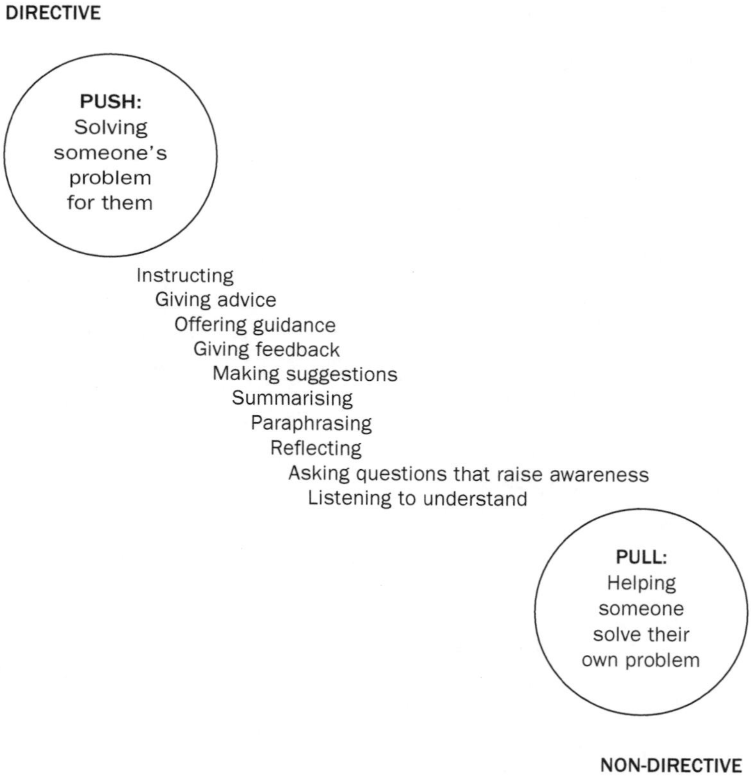

DIRECTIVE

PUSH:
Solving
someone's
problem
for them

Instructing
Giving advice
Offering guidance
Giving feedback
Making suggestions
Summarising
Paraphrasing
Reflecting
Asking questions that raise awareness
Listening to understand

PULL:
Helping
someone
solve their
own problem

NON-DIRECTIVE

Thus behaviours such as instructing, offering advice and giving feedback are at the directive end, while listening, questioning and reflecting are at the non-directive end. I find that there is usually considerable agreement on this, but more debate on the differences between summarising, paraphrasing and reflecting. We will consider this in more detail in Chapter 4 when we look at the skill of playing back to the client what they have said, which can be done in all three of these ways.

The figure also suggests that when you are coaching in a more directive style, you are more likely to be looking to solve someone's problem for them or to *push* them towards a solution that you have in mind. On the other hand, when coaching non-directively, your role is to help the other person to find their own solutions or to *pull* the ideas from them.

Directive and non-directive approaches

Being clear about your position on being directive or non-directive will help you in the moment to clarify your intent when deciding what to do next within a coaching session. While it is possible to take an extreme position, and indeed some counsellors would seek to operate exclusively at the non-directive end, in practice many coaches will operate at different points on the spectrum in different situations. If you are willing to vary your approach in different situations, it helps to do this with a conscious awareness of what you are doing and what your intention is.

In their book *The Reflecting Glass: Professional Coaching for Leadership Development*, Lucy West and Mike Milan open by considering three types of coaching which fall along a continuum from training to development (Figure 1.2).

Figure 1.2 Types of coaching

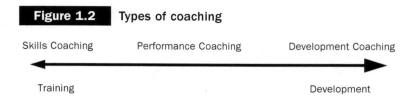

For them, skills coaching sits at the directive end where the coach is 'effectively training the client' to develop specific skills.

Somewhere in the middle, performance coaching has a wider purpose to enhance the client's performance more generally in their current role.

At the non-directive end, development coaching is about creating 'the conditions for reflective learning'. A coach does this, they say:

> by first creating a psychological space, which allows the executive to stand back from the workplace, and then providing a supportive, yet challenging, relationship and dialogue in which the executive can gain perspective on his or her experiences and self, and on his or her leadership task within the organisation. (West and Milan, 2001)

In *Effective Coaching*, Myles Downey states his belief that it is impossible for the coach to be completely non-directive 'because the slightest flicker of concern in the eye, the faintest smile of approval will show up and be read and interpreted by the player' (by *player* he means the person being coached). He also writes that there will be times when the client is stuck and you can be of most help by offering some feedback or advice at the directive end. 'However', he says, 'the magic inhabits the non-directive end of the spectrum'.

Where you wish to operate along the spectrum from directive to non-directive in your coaching practice is very important, and we will look at this in more detail in Chapter 6 on directive and non-directive coaching.

Coaching or mentoring?

I am often asked what the difference is between coaching and mentoring. My usual answer is that until you define your terms they mean the same thing. Here is an illustration of how the words are used differently by leading firms in the field. When I worked for Transco, one aspect of my role was to commission external coaching for some of our directors and senior managers. I mainly used two excellent organisations, CPS and Praesta (then called The Change Partnership).

The CPS website describes what they do in the following words:

> With person-centred issues, our skill lies in our ability to help individuals, through mentoring, to gain deeper insight into their own behaviour and interaction with others; to recognise, accept and adapt established, unconscious patterns of behaviour that can inhibit personal performance. The mentor plays the role of probe and challenger of the client's thinking to allow his/her own solutions and insights to emerge.
>
> From time to time, when an individual may be experiencing a particularly difficult period, counselling may be required with a focus on developing coping strategies.
>
> If the focus of the work is role and/or task-oriented, a coaching approach, where we offer specific advice

and guidance, may be more appropriate. For example, when an individual is taking up a new appointment and needs to understand what is required from his/her new role. (See *www.cps-ltd.co.uk/services/*)

On the other hand, the Praesta website says the following:

> A Praesta coach acts as a sounding board; challenges thinking; stimulates creativity; provides tools and techniques for dealing with situations; gives encouragement; and builds confidence.
>
> The coach has unconditional positive regard for the client, has no agenda other than the client's and is always on the client's side. Together with good personal chemistry – which is essential – this builds a working partnership based on trust.
>
> Every client gets the benefit of fresh thinking as well as deep experience...
>
> As a result of the coaching experience, clients develop their potential and apply it productively in the workplace. (See *www.praesta.com/international/ workingwithpraesta.html*)

As the quotes indicate, what CPS calls *mentoring* is called *coaching* by Praesta. Personally, I use the words *coaching* and *mentoring* in the opposite way to CPS. For me, mentoring is more likely to be a situation where a more experienced person helps another to work out their way forward, in part by sharing their experience, offering suggestions and giving advice. These are behaviours at the more directive end of the spectrum, and they may be entirely appropriate depending on the context and the agreed objectives of the mentoring arrangement. In advocating a predominantly non-directive approach in this book, I am not claiming that this is the only way in which someone might help another to perform, learn or develop.

Here is a definition of mentoring that I have coined to parallel the definition of coaching offered earlier in the chapter:

> Mentoring occurs through a series of conversations in which one person draws on their experience, expertise and knowledge to advise and guide a less experienced person in order to enhance their performance or support their development.

Awareness and responsibility

There is one other idea I'd like to introduce in this opening chapter, and it goes to the heart of what you are trying to do in coaching non-directively. In their workshops to help managers and others learn the basics of coaching, John Whitmore and his colleagues at Performance Consultants summarise what an effective coach is seeking to achieve in the following equation:

$$Awareness + Responsibility = Performance$$

In other words, to coach effectively you are trying to do two things – to help the other person to become more aware of what they need to do and how to do it, and to encourage them to take responsibility for acting. The fundamental premise is that someone who is aware of what to do and who takes responsibility will perform effectively – whatever performance means in their context. It might be delivering excellent customer service, leading a sales team, hitting a golf ball well, and so on.

In workshops, John Whitmore used to add that *awareness without responsibility is just whingeing*. In other words, someone who is well aware of what they need to do about an issue but who takes no responsibility for acting is simply whingeing. We will look at this again in Chapter 5 on becoming a capable coach.

In *Coaching for Performance*, Whitmore writes that, while the GROW model is an effective way of structuring a coaching conversation, awareness and responsibility are more important ideas. He urges his readers: 'If you get anything at all out of this book, let it be AWARENESS and RESPONSIBILITY, not G R O W'. In his view, 'Building Awareness and Responsibility is the essence of good coaching'.

2

Listening

Introduction

For a number of years when I ran workshops to help participants develop their coaching skills, I took the view that two basic skills were needed to coach successfully – the ability to listen well and the ability to ask effective questions. More recently, reflecting on what I actually do when I am coaching, I have come to the view that there are actually three basic skills – listening, questioning and playing back. By playing back, I mean feeding back to the client what they have said in one of three ways – summarising, paraphrasing and reflecting back using the client's own words. You might take the view that playing back is an important aspect of listening, but I am increasingly of the opinion that it is worthy of being considered a separate skill. In the next three chapters I would like to look at these three skills in turn. In reality, of course, a capable coach uses these skills in an integrated way as they converse with their client – for instance, the question you ask or the summary that you play back depends very much on what you have heard and observed as a listener.

In this chapter, then, I'd like to explore what it means to listen well. We will look at the different ways in which people listen to one another, identify the quality of listening necessary to coach effectively, and explore why it is important as a coach to listen. We will also consider the place of silence in coaching.

Levels of listening

There are different ways of listening to someone, most of which are unsuitable for coaching. First, and it is not an uncommon experience, is *not listening at all*. On workshops I sometimes use an exercise where I ask people to pair up and invite one person in each pair to speak for one minute on something that interests them, while the other person has to demonstrate that they aren't listening. A number of things usually occur. First, the 'listeners' nearly always use non-verbal means to demonstrate that they aren't listening – looking away, yawning or even sometimes walking off. Second, the experience of not being listened to is very disconcerting for the speakers. A minute spent in this way seems a very long time, and people often dry up before the minute is over – and this on a topic that interests them! Third, when I call time there is generally a lot of noise in the room as the tension that has built up – in only 60 seconds – is released. The exercise is a very quick and powerful way of demonstrating that not being listened to is a bad experience.

A second and pretty common way of listening is *listening, waiting to speak*. This is when I want to talk and will wait for as short a time as possible before starting to speak. Sometimes I might wait for you to pause, but equally I might interrupt you in mid-sentence. In *Life Together*, Dietrich Bonhoeffer describes this kind of attention as 'listening with half an ear':

> Anyone who cannot listen long and patiently will presently be talking beside the point and be never really

speaking to others. There is a kind of listening with half an ear that presumes already to know what the other person has to say. It is an impatient, inattentive listening, that despises the brother and is only waiting for a chance to speak and thus get rid of the other person. (Quoted in Shaw, 2005)

A third way of listening – and it is typical of the kind of listening that goes on in many meetings – is *listening to disagree*. I want my point of view to prevail or to get my way. I'm listening for the weak points in what you say, and when I spot one I pounce. In some situations – in a court of law or in much academic discourse – this is the normal form of conversation, and it may be entirely appropriate. It is about debate and argument. It is about winning and losing, or perhaps compromising. Indeed, some of the language we use to describe this form of conversation reveals its essentially adversarial nature – *I attack your position, I defend my views, I overcome your reservations, I probe for the weak points in your argument, I win the case, I lose the argument.* In Chapter 10 we look at the power of metaphors. The underlying metaphor here is that argument is war.

A fourth type of listening – and this way of listening is vital if you want to coach well – is *listening to understand*. In *Effective Coaching*, Myles Downey puts it this way: 'In coaching the purpose of listening is to understand, because that in turn generates understanding and awareness in the player' (by *player* he means *client*).

In listening to understand, I am trying to see the world as it appears through your eyes. I am trying to appreciate what you are thinking and how you are feeling. I want to understand your dreams and your hopes, your fears and your doubts. The word that is often used here is *empathy*.

Note that empathy is not the same as sympathy. My colleague, Shirley Crookes, describes the difference in the following way. When I sympathise with you, I am imagining how *I* would feel if I were in your shoes. When I empathise, I imagine how *you* feel in your shoes.

In this type of listening, it is important that you somehow communicate your understanding to the client. One way to convey this is by playing back to the client your understanding, and in Chapter 4 we will look at the use of summary, paraphrase and reflection to do this. Sometimes simply playing back to the client what they have just said can help to deepen their understanding of their situation.

If I can appreciate how the world seems to you, I will ask you better and more useful questions, questions that take your thinking forward. Questioning and listening go hand in hand. If I am coaching you well, my questions will emerge from what you tell me.

Moreover, in listening to you I show you respect, and this helps to build the relationship between us. This is vital because coaching is, as we defined it in the opening chapter, primarily a relationship. In *Turning to One Another*, Margaret Wheatley writes: 'Why is being heard so healing? I don't know the full answer to that question, but I do know that it has something to do with the fact that listening creates relationship'. This is a tremendously important point. Simply listening to another person nurtures the relationship between you.

Beyond listening to understand there is another way of listening that is helpful in coaching – *listening to help the client to understand*. Remember that in coaching you are trying to help your client to become more aware and to encourage them to take responsibility. In *The Coach's Coach*, Alison Hardingham writes that, 'The coach is listening to the coachee's story in order to develop the coachee's self-awareness and increase her resourcefulness to solve problems at work in the present'. As long as your client understands, you don't have to know what they are thinking. In any case, you won't fully understand their reality in all its complexity and subtlety anyway.

The silent coaching exercise that we looked at in the opening chapter demonstrates that you can help someone without even knowing what their issue is. I once coached someone from Beijing whose accent meant that it was difficult for me to grasp all that he was saying. He in turn found it difficult to understand me when I was speaking. But by continuing to show him respect and to pay close attention to him, I believe that I was able to help him think through his situation in ways that were meaningful to him. It didn't matter that I didn't fully understand.

In *Time to Think*, Nancy Kline has a superb chapter called 'Attention', which is all about listening. She speaks of the

Figure 2.1   Levels of listening

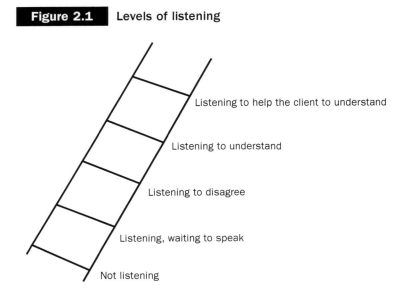

Listening to help the client to understand

Listening to understand

Listening to disagree

Listening, waiting to speak

Not listening

times when the client might go quiet as they think deeply about something. She writes: 'Listening to their quiet, you will not know *what* they are thinking. But you will know *that* they are thinking....ideas are forming, insights are melding, most of which you will never hear about' (Kline, 1999).

Figure 2.1 summarises these five different levels of listening.

Listening with the head, the heart and the gut

In this section I'd like to consider listening in different ways from another perspective. We will assume that you are listening in order to understand your client. Within that mode of listening you can listen with your head, your heart and your gut. Let me explain what is meant by these metaphors.

First, *listening with your head* means focusing on the words that your client actually says. At a thinking level, they are communicating facts, information, arguments, ideas and concepts. You might imagine that they are communicating from their head to your head, and you may speak back from your head to their head.

However, people communicate at a feelings level too. They may vocalise their feelings – *I'm angry, I feel sad, This is so exciting*, etc. Often, however, the words spoken may be only the tip of the iceberg and the feelings that lie beneath the words may be expressed non-verbally – through tone of voice, body language or facial expression. To listen effectively you need to tune into what is not being said. You might call listening at a feelings level *listening with your heart*.

At a deeper level still, you might *listen with your gut* – that is, with your intuition – and pick up messages that are there but again are not spoken. Sometimes your gut tells you things well before your intellect catches on. With your gut, you might hear about your client's fears or hopes or needs.

Figure 2.2 illustrates these three levels of listening using the metaphor of an iceberg. Above the surface you pick up with your head the words that are actually said. Below the surface you pick up with your heart and your gut what is not said – the emotions, fears, hopes and so on.

Playing back what you hear with your heart or your intuition requires you to be more tentative than playing back the words that you hear with your head. You might preface your remarks to indicate that they are somewhat provisional. For instance, you might say things like:

- It sounds to me as though you're feeling angry.

- My guess is that you're upset about this.

- I'm not sure, but I'm wondering if what you actually want is a new job.

- It occurs to me that you may be asking yourself if you want to stay in this relationship.

I sometimes use an expression such *as Let me say what's going through my mind just now* when I want to say

Figure 2.2 **The iceberg model of listening**

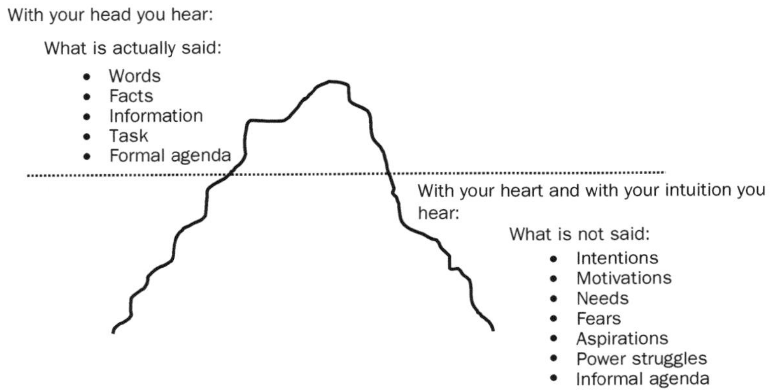

With your head you hear:

What is actually said:
- Words
- Facts
- Information
- Task
- Formal agenda

With your heart and with your intuition you hear:

What is not said:
- Intentions
- Motivations
- Needs
- Fears
- Aspirations
- Power struggles
- Informal agenda

something with a degree of tentativeness that is intended to give the client freedom to agree or disagree or clarify or expand.

One way in which you might get in touch with what you are picking up with your heart or your gut is by paying attention to what is happening to your body. It may be, for instance, that you develop tension in your neck or shoulders, or your stomach may become agitated, or you may find yourself stifling a yawn. There might well be clues here as to what is going on for the client. Depending on the client and the degree of rapport between you, you might choose to share your experience directly with them – for example, by saying something along the lines of *I'm noticing that as you speak I'm feeling tension in my neck and shoulders.* Give the client space to respond as they wish – or indeed not to respond.

In *The 7 Habits of Highly Effective People*, Stephen Covey makes the point that to listen well requires emotional strength:

> To relate effectively with a wife, a husband, children, friends, or working associates, we must learn to listen. And this requires emotional strength. Listening involves patience, openness, and the desire to understand – highly developed qualities of character. It's so much easier to operate from a low emotional level and to give high-level advice. (Covey, 1989)

I have also come across the metaphor of *listening for the feet*. This means listening for your client's intentions, motivation or will. What do they actually want and what will they actually do? Often they are not clear or even aware of what they want. Again, listening at this level may involve listening for what is not vocalised.

Silence

An important aspect of some coaching conversations is silence. There are different kinds of silence. In *Dialogue and the Art of Thinking Together*, Bill Isaacs writes of four types of silence that may be experienced in a group:

- *awkward* silences, where people feel uncomfortable;
- *tense* silences, where there is disagreement and conflict;
- *thoughtful* silences, where people are reflecting and looking inwards;
- *sacred* silences, where wisdom has replaced chatter.

A key challenge in your development as a coach is learning to be comfortable with silence, particularly thoughtful or sacred types of silence. If your client is busy thinking, why on earth would you want to break the silence? When the silence is awkward or tense, you need to consider whether and how to break the silence – with a question, a playback, an exercise or a comment in the here and now about the silence. Being clear about your intention is important before you break a silence. Breaking a silence simply because you feel uncomfortable is not appropriate. Breaking a silence because your client seems to be feeling uncomfortable may or may not be appropriate.

In *Fierce Conversations*, Susan Scott writes of her work as an executive coach that:

> During my conversations with the people most important to me, silence has become my favourite sound, because that is when the work is being done. Of all the tools I use during conversations and all the principles I keep in mind, silence is the most powerful of all. (Scott 2002)

These sentiments are echoed by Nancy Kline when talking about the quiet times when the client is busy thinking: 'These quiet busy times are when the least *seems* to be happening but the most *is* happening. I think they are now my favourite moments in listening to people think.' Faced with silence when your client is working, *don't just do something, sit there!*

Active, attentive listening

Listening is hard work. If you have ever spent a day conducting recruitment interviews, you probably have some sense of this. Listening requires concentration. It calls for skill to do it well. It may be emotionally draining. I frequently feel very tired after listening. However, it is a tiredness that often goes along with a feeling of satisfaction if I think my listening has been helpful to the client.

In *A Heart to Listen*, Michael Mitton writes:

> Attentive listening is creating space – it is constructive. It is not sitting passively in front of a verbal water jet. It is actively applying often intense concentration to facilitate the person we are listening to, to help them move on in their journey. (Quoted in Shaw, 2005)

This kind of listening is often referred to as *active listening*. Alison Hardingham lists three reasons why the word *active* is appropriate:

- the listener is doing things;
- while it is going on, changes are happening;
- it takes effort and application to do well.

The other adjective that I like to describe the quality of listening needed to coach well is *attentive*. Nancy Kline describes attention as 'the art of listening with palpable respect and fascination'. She writes, 'The quality of your attention determines the quality of other people's thinking'. She adds that, 'Giving good attention to people makes them more intelligent. Poor attention makes them stumble over their words and seem stupid. Your attention, your listening is that important.'

Why listening is so important

One lesson I have taken from my experiences over the years in coaching people is that I am more effective as a coach when I listen with genuine interest to the other person and their story. This effectiveness is at two levels. I ask more useful questions and play back more accurate summaries when I listen well. But, more importantly, I feel that I create a more meaningful coaching relationship when I listen to a client with attention, with respect and non-judgmentally.

I want to emphasise these two linked but distinct reasons why it is so important for a coach to listen well to a client. First, in order to respond with an appropriate question or intervention or silence, you need to understand the client's world – their reality, their hopes, their aspirations, their fears and the things that are stopping them from taking action. Alison Hardingham says that, in her view, active listening:

> is the single most important skill for a coach. It is what enables the coach to understand the coachee and her world. Every other intervention the coach makes has to

be based on that understanding, and the more complete that understanding is, the more effectively the coach will intervene. (Hardingham 2004)

This might seem a good enough reason to claim that listening is vital to good coaching. However, the second reason is even more fundamental. Listening, as Margaret Wheatley says, creates relationship, and good coaching is first and foremost about the relationship between you and your client. Myles Downey writes that, 'Without a relationship there is no coaching. In fact the only real mistake that a coach can make is to damage the relationship irreparably.'

A useful way of developing your ability to listen attentively is to cultivate a genuine interest in other people and their stories. In *Growing People* I wrote that, 'In conversation the opposite of curiosity is certainty. When you are certain you understand the other person's point of view, you stop inquiring and you probably also stop listening.' You can practise your listening skills simply by being genuinely interested in another person and what they might be trying to communicate, both in words and non-verbally.

Listening and being non-directive

Nancy Kline (1999) compares poor listening, on the one hand, and attentive listening, on the other. Most of the time, she says, 'We think we listen, but we don't. We finish each other's sentences, we interrupt each other, we moan ... We give advice, give advice, give advice.' In contrast to giving advice and ideas, she writes that:

> Real help is different. Real help, personally or professionally, consists of listening to people, of paying

respectful attention to people so that they can *access their own ideas first*. Usually the brain that contains the problem also contains the solution – often the best one. When you keep that in mind, you become more effective with people. And people around you end up with better ideas. (Kline, 1999, author's emphasis)

So, while listening is important in all forms of coaching, listening with respect and attention is especially and fundamentally important in non-directive coaching.

3

Questioning

Introduction

If attentive listening is the most important skill you need to coach well, then questioning is the next most important. In this chapter, we will consider various aspects of asking questions. We will look at the difference between open and closed questions, and consider other kinds of question that you might ask as a coach.

Listening and questioning

Listening and questioning go hand in hand – good coaching questions emerge from listening to the client with empathy and curiosity. Alison Hardingham reckons that 'Questioning … together with active listening probably achieves 80% of the positive outcome of coaching'.

A good coaching question is one that makes the client think. For example, they may think more deeply about something they have just said, or they may think through the consequences of a possible action, or they may face up to some contradiction in what they have been saying.

If the challenge in coaching is represented in terms of the equation:

$$Awareness + Responsibility = Performance$$

then a useful question will either raise awareness or encourage responsibility.

Asking a question to which the client already knows the answer is not helpful. For instance if your client says his wife has just left him, asking *Oh, what is her name?* is not a useful question. Sometimes, you need an appreciation of the context and some details to help understand where your client is coming from, although you may be surprised how often you don't actually need to know. The silent coaching exercise is a powerful demonstration that your questions can be helpful even when you do not actually know what the issue is.

In his book *The Skilled Helper*, Gerard Egan talks about how inexperienced or inept counsellors may ask too many questions or questions that add no value. He writes that, 'many clients instinctively know when questions are just filler, used because the helper does not have anything better to say. I have caught myself asking questions the answers to which I didn't even want to know.'

John Whitmore warns of the danger of the coach working out the next question to ask while the client is still speaking. He writes that:

> If the coach is working out the next question while the coachee is speaking, the coachee will be aware that he is not really listening. Far better to hear the person through and then pause if necessary while the next appropriate question comes to mind. (Whitmore, 2002)

One of the things that learner coaches find difficult is this ability not to worry about what they are going to say next. This is particularly true if they are still becoming familiar with the GROW model and following its steps in a somewhat mechanistic way. The challenge for the learner coach is to develop the confidence simply to listen and trust that their next question or statement will emerge when it is required. Myles Downey offers some words to encourage the coach to let go and trust the process:

> If you are completely focused and interested in your player's learning, your natural instinct to coach ... will manifest, and you will ask an appropriate question. In any case it does not particularly matter if you make a mistake. Coaching is not an exam where you get one chance. If a question does not work, ask another. (Downey, 2003)

In the previous chapter we noted that one way of developing your listening skills is to cultivate a genuine interest in other people and their stories. This is also a useful way of developing your questioning skills. Alison Hardingham writes that:

> We develop our questioning skill best by developing our capacity for curiosity. Encourage yourself to wonder, about all kinds of people and all kinds of situation. Ask yourself lots of questions, and you will become better at asking them of other people. (Hardingham, 2004)

Open and closed questions

In thinking about the kinds of question you might ask as a coach, it is very useful to distinguish between open and closed questions. Open questions usually begin with Kipling's trusted friends:

I keep six honest serving-men
(They taught me all I knew);
Their names are *What* and *Why* and *When*
And *How* and *Where* and *Who*.

Closed questions, interestingly, always begin with a verb:

- Have you ...?

- Are you ...?

- Could you ...?

- Will you ...?

Open questions are generally more useful than closed ones because they prompt more thinking in the client and so are more likely either to raise their awareness or to encourage responsibility. A closed question can usually be answered simply with a yes or no or another one-word answer, often with little thought required. Gerard Egan observes that, 'Counselors who ask closed questions find themselves asking more and more questions. One closed question begets another.'

A closed question can generally be easily turned into an equivalent but more thought-provoking open question. For example, imagine how someone might answer the set of alternative questions shown in Table 3.1.

You may be lucky and find that the client interprets a closed question as an open one, and gives an expansive answer, but it is safer to ask the open question in the first place.

Occasionally, a closed question is just what is called for. For instance, you may want to check out if your client really is committed to an action by asking a question such as: *So, will you speak to your boss today?* Or, you may deliberately want to challenge your client's thinking by asking, for

| Table 3.1 | Closed and open questions |

Closed	Open
Was it the signal which caused the accident?	What caused the accident?
Have you finished?	How close are you to finishing?
Do you like the new job?	What do you like about the new job?
Are you supportive?	How supportive are you?

example, *So, is resigning from your job what you really want?*

A word of caution about asking a question beginning with *why* – this can often come across as unduly challenging and might provoke defensiveness in the client. Myles Downey warns that, 'The *why* question more often than not elicits reasons, justifications and excuses, not one of which is useful in raising awareness'.

A helpful idea if you want to challenge your client but are concerned that you may come across as overly critical or judgmental is the notion of *softening* the question. You might, for instance, ask a *why* type of question in one of the following ways:

- I was wondering what was going through your mind when you decided to do that.

- I'm interested in your reasons for saying that.

- What do you think that will achieve?

- What is it that makes this important for you?

Note too that these examples not only soften the question but may also give it a more specific focus than a more general *why* question.

Crisp questions

The word I like to use to describe the right question is *crisp*. A crisp question – simply expressed – helps to focus the client on the most useful issue for them at that moment in time. Note that this is more art than science. I could never prove that another question or another phrasing of a question would not have been better still. Sometimes I just know – or occasionally the client will tell me – that I have asked a really useful question.

A common mistake made by people learning coaching skills is to ask questions that are not at all crisp. One way that they do this is by asking a number of questions all rolled into one. For instance:

> What are you going to do about that? I mean, are you going to speak to him? Or, have you thought of sending an e-mail? What would be the best way forward? What would make the most difference?

There are five questions here. Any one of them might be a really useful question, although two of them are closed questions and possibly might even be leading questions. Often, if the learner coach simply left it at the first question, it would be a good question. In this case, simply asking *What are you going to do about that?* and waiting for the answer might be really helpful.

I encourage you to notice the questions that you ask and, in particular, to consider how many words it takes you to ask a question. It is often possible to ask a helpful, crisp question in no more than half a dozen words. You may, of course, wish to preface a question with some acknowledgment of what the client has just said. But when you do ask your question, how many words are you using?

Other types of question

A statement such as *What on earth did you do that for?* is not really a question. Just because there is a question mark at the end does not make it a question in coaching.

On the other hand, a statement such as *Tell me more about...* is, in coaching, effectively a very open question, an invitation to the client to think.

A question beginning with *What else...* can often be a good question to encourage more thinking in the client. For example, a generally useful question when exploring the reality phase of the GROW model is *What else is relevant?* Alternatively, when exploring options you might ask *What else might you do?* I do sometimes find, however, that a client thinks I am suggesting they have missed something specific when I ask this question, and I need to clarify that I don't have an answer in mind. And I did have one client who told me that he hated my *What else...* questions.

When your client makes a statement that is somewhat vague or fuzzy, a *clarifying* question can help them to refine their thinking. As an illustration, a client might say something along the lines of *I'm fed up with all of this.* To help the client become more aware of their situation and their feelings, it may help to ask a clarifying question such as *What exactly are you fed up with?*

You can use a *probing* question to encourage the client to think more deeply (for instance, *What is really going on?*); or to be more precise (such as, *What specifically are you going to do?*); or to face up to a possible contradiction in what they have been saying (for instance, *In what way does your desire to do X fit with your concern for Y?*).

Alison Hardingham uses *differentiating* questions to encourage deeper reflection. She suggests using questions such as:

- What is the most difficult part of your role?
- Who is the best example of that?
- What is the strongest reason for change?

Using words such as *most*, *best* and *strongest* invites the client to compare and contrast. Hence, the client is often unable to answer immediately, and this type of question promotes a mood of reflection.

You may sometimes ask a *hypothetical* question to encourage your client to explore possibilities. *What might happen if…?* For instance, you might ask a client who had ruled out a number of possible options because they couldn't drive: *If you had passed your driving test, what would you like to do?* A specific question that you might sometimes ask to free up a client's thinking about what is possible is: *What is the worst that could happen?*

Reframing

Another useful type of question aims to help the client *reframe* their situation, that is, to see their situation in a new way. Alison Hardingham writes that, 'Reframing is changing the meaning of something by putting it in a different context'. She gives the example of a teenage boy who is continually arguing with his mother. If the mother views this as a lack of respect for her, she may well become angry. If she reframes this as her son coping with the difficulties of adolescence, she may feel compassion instead. These different feelings are likely to lead to different behaviours in response.

Reframing can be particularly helpful when a client is stuck. In their book *Co-Active Coaching*, Laura Whitworth, Henry Kimsey-House and Phil Sandahl write that:

Frequently clients get stuck with a certain way of looking at a situation or experience. Their perspective, moreover, has a message that is in some way disabling. Your ability to reframe the experience in a new way provides a fresh perspective and a sense of renewed possibility. (Whitworth, Kimsey-House and Sandahl, 1998)

As an illustration, imagine a client who is facing redundancy and is focusing exclusively on everything they are going to lose as a result. Without attempting to minimise the depth of their concerns or the difficulties ahead, asking a question such as *What possibilities would this open up for you?* might help them to look at their prospects in a different and more constructive way.

Leading questions

A leading question is one that already contains the answer, or at least a suggested answer. John Whitmore writes that, 'Leading questions, the resort of many poor coaches, indicate that the coach does not believe in what he is attempting to do'.

Learner coaches frequently ask questions that are really suggestions, along the lines of *Do you think it would be a good idea to...?* There are a number of possible reasons for this. First, the learner coach who is trying to help their client and who is beginning to understand some of the client's world will see possible ways forward and offer suggestions in the honest belief that this will be useful. Second, the learner coach may feel uncomfortable listening to someone talk about an unresolved issue or problem – offering a solution seems a way of making things better for the client and removing the discomfort that both may be feeling. Third, the learner coach may not yet be confident or capable enough to ask good questions or tolerate a silence.

You may find that you sometimes ask a question expecting the client to give a particular answer, and you might even experience some sense of disappointment if the answer is not as you expected. Although you may not be leading the client, notice that you have some attachment to the answer. A really useful notion that I came across in a conversation about coaching with Catherine Joyce is to *ask the question without any attachment to the answer*. In other words, be completely open-minded about how the client might reply, and work with whatever they communicate.

Incisive questions

Nancy Kline describes a specific approach that involves asking what she terms *incisive* questions. In this section I'd like to summarise the approach. There may be aspects that you can assimilate in your own practice. For example, after reading her book I added *What assumptions are you making?* to my list of silent coaching questions. However, if you really want to employ the methodology of incisive questions, then it is worth looking in detail at her book *Time to Think*. You can also find information about workshops to learn about using this approach on the website *www.timetothink.com*.

An incisive question 'removes the barrier that is stopping the person from thinking further'. She writes:

> An Incisive Question, crafted with precision and lustre, is any question that removes limiting assumptions from your thinking so that you can think again. An Incisive

Question does this by replacing the limiting assumption with a freeing one. (Kline, 1999)

She goes on to describe different types of limiting assumptions, which she calls facts, possible-facts and bedrock assumptions. She then explains how to design the appropriate incisive question. The coach first helps the client to articulate in their own words:

- the goal that they want to achieve;
- the limiting assumption that is holding them back from doing what they want or need to do;
- a freeing assumption that is the positive opposite of their limiting assumption.

The coach then asks:

- an incisive question inviting the client to think about what they would do if they believed the freeing assumption.

She offers some examples of incisive questions based on freeing assumptions:

- If you knew that you are intelligent, how would you talk to your boss?
- If you could trust that your children would be fine, what would you do with the rest of your life?
- If you knew that you are vital to this organisation's success, how would you approach your work?

The form of these questions is:

If you knew + freeing assumption + client's goal = incisive question

The freeing assumption needs to be stated in positive terms and uses the exact language of the client. It is the client, not the coach, who identifies what they see as the positive alternative to their limiting assumption. The freeing assumption, she argues, also needs to be stated in the present tense.

Kline places great emphasis on the wording – of the goal as well as the assumptions – coming from the client. She writes that, 'The best wording is the Thinker's own: their mind has specifically chosen and uttered those exact words for a reason'. We will explore the importance of using the client's exact words in Chapter 10 when we consider the notion of clean language.

She recommends that you ask the incisive question repeatedly because each time you ask you will hear a fresh idea from the client until they run out of ideas. It is also worth writing down the exact form of the incisive question – often the client will find the same question useful in different situations.

What do you do when you don't know what question to ask?

David Whitaker, coach of the UK team that won the men's hockey gold medal at the 1988 Olympics, offers the following guideline to help when you are unsure what to say next in a coaching conversation: *If in doubt, build the relationship*. In his view, anything that develops the relationship between yourself and your client can only help. For example, playing back an empathic understanding of the client and their world is likely to build the relationship.

Myles Downey echoes this when he writes that, 'There is only one mistake that you can make in coaching and that is to irreparably damage the relationship'.

Another approach, which is likely to be more suitable when your client understands the coaching process, is simply to ask them *What is the most helpful question I could ask you now?* You might preface this by acknowledging that you are not sure what to do next.

One thing that I sometimes do when I'm not sure what to do next is to offer a summary of where I think we are up to in the conversation, or perhaps ask the client to summarise where we are. One benefit of a summary is simply that it gives you time to think. Chapter 4 will look at playing what the client has said back to them.

You might combine these ideas by summarising, indicating some possible ways of taking the conversation forward, and inviting the client to choose what they would like to do next in the session. For example, you might respond to a client along the lines:

> There seem to be three aspects of the situation that are important to you: X, Y and Z. We probably have time to look at just one of these today. Which one would you like to explore?

Questioning and being non-directive

I had a very interesting experience when I was running the Certificate in Coaching at the University of Warwick. One of the participants on the programme had a lot of experience working as a counsellor, using primarily a Rogerian non-directive approach. Many learner coaches find it difficult to ask good questions because they are far more accustomed to offering advice or making suggestions. This participant found it difficult to ask questions for a completely different reason. For her, asking questions was too directive. Her usual approach when counselling was mainly to play back to her client what they had said or communicated non-verbally. She might also share with the client how she was experiencing their encounter, perhaps saying something along the lines of: *It seems to me that you're feeling really stuck.*

Working with her gave me considerable food for thought, challenging my own approach which I would describe as primarily non-directive. In asking a question, or in choosing what to ask the question about, or in wording the question in a certain way, I am necessarily being selective in what I focus on and thus am directing the conversation. When I introduce a concept or an exercise, I am again directing the conversation. As such, I very much structure the conversation. In my view, a key part of my role as a coach is to manage the conversation – in the best interests of the client, I hope. I aim, at the same time, to be primarily non-directive in terms of not giving advice or steering the client in a particular direction. In summary, I aim to be non-directive about the content but I am often directive about the process.

I would therefore encourage you, as you develop your coaching skills and style, to consider this issue of how directive you want to be in structuring the conversation as well as how directive you want to be in guiding your clients.

4

Playing back

Introduction

In this short chapter I would like to explore the skill of playing back to the client what they have said or perhaps communicated non-verbally. This is sometimes regarded as an aspect of listening, but I think it warrants being considered as a separate skill and behaviour when used by an effective coach.

Three ways of playing back to the client

I use three main ways of playing back to the client my understanding of what they have said. First, I will *summarise* my understanding of the key points. I might, for instance, say something like *You seem to be saying that there are three issues here...* Or I might say *So far you've identified two options...* I will often use a summary to cover an extended piece of conversation.

Second, I will *paraphrase* what the client has said, turning their words into a different formulation. For instance, the client might say *It feels like I'm banging my head against a brick wall*, and I might respond with *It sounds like you're feeling very frustrated and perhaps a bit angry.*

Third, I will *reflect back* to the client what they have said, repeating their exact words. In a moment we'll look why it might be very important to repeat the specific words used by the client. In the previous illustration, for example, I might respond with *Tell me more about what it's like to be banging your head against a brick wall.* Alternatively, there might be a single word that seems pregnant with significance, perhaps indicated by the client's tone of voice. To illustrate, the client might say *I'm very disappointed with my boss's response,* with an emphasis on the word *disappointed.* To which I might just say in an inquisitive tone, *Disappointed?* Or I might say, *And what's behind 'disappointed'?*

There are a number of possible benefits from playing back to the client your understanding of what they've communicated. First, if your playback is reasonably accurate, it conveys that you have listened and understood what they have been saying. Second, it lets you check and possibly amend your understanding. The client might respond with *No, that isn't quite what I mean...* Third, it may allow the client to amend their own understanding – they might, for instance, respond with *Mmmm, now that I think about it, I'm only really concerned about John's reaction not Mary's.* Or they might say, *Actually, there's something else that's important here.*

Myles Downey says of these three skills:

> In using these skills something special can happen. As the coach repeats what has been said, summarises, or paraphrases, the player often has a new insight or idea. I can only guess as to why that might happen. I think it is that, as the player hears the issue played back, it is possible to get a little distance ... from the issue, to be not so attached, and in seeing it differently to have some new thoughts. (Downey, 2003)

Using the client's exact words

In a chapter in *Excellence in Coaching*, Frank Bresser and Carol Wilson say that 'Reflecting back the coachee's exact words is one of the most powerful tools in coaching ... coachees receive a boost when they hear their own words coming from someone else.'

There are a number of coaches and therapists who take the view that it is vital to use the exact words of the client and that to modify their words introduces unhelpful distortions. For example, in the previous chapter we noted how Nancy Kline emphasises that in framing an incisive question it is important to employ the client's precise statement of their goal and of their positive, freeing assumption. She says that, 'With hardly an exception the Thinker's word is fresher, more accurate for them, more exactly right than any I would have thought of' (Kline, 1999).

The importance of using the client's exact words and metaphors is central to the work of James Lawley and Penny Tompkins (2000). They use the notion of *clean language* to ask questions that employ the exact words and metaphors used by the client. They believe that there is a power and richness in the metaphors used by a client. If the coach rewords what the client says, this introduces a different model of the world. We will look at this in some detail in Chapter 10 on metaphors and clean language.

Managing the conversation

One of your key responsibilities as a coach is to manage the conversation. What a coach does to manage a coaching session depends on what the client needs at different points in the conversation. It also depends on your own style of coaching, and where you stand on the spectrum from being directive to being non-directive as a coach. In one situation, it might be appropriate to say virtually nothing for ten minutes as your client works effectively without any prompting from you. At another time, you might need to ask questions, perhaps using the GROW model as a framework. Sometimes, you might suggest that your client carries out an exercise such as drawing a picture or sorting a set of value cards to identify which values are most important to them in a job. (Exercises such as these will be considered in Chapter 8.)

In my own practice, one of the key ways in which I manage a coaching conversation is to play back to the client what I have heard. The use of summary, paraphrase and reflection are ways to punctuate the conversation. This gives the client the opportunity to look again at their situation, and it gives the coach space to consider what to do next.

Frank Bresser and Carol Wilson also suggest that summarising can be a polite way of interrupting a client who is 'bogged down in story telling and detail'. This then lets you focus the conversation where you consider it will be of more benefit to the talkative client.

Another way in which you might manage the conversation is to invite the client to summarise. This lets them pick out what is most significant for them, which might be different from what you would have highlighted. While asking the client to summarise does not convey your understanding, it lets them clarify their thinking. You might, for instance, say something like *We've covered a lot of ground today – what are the key points for you?* Or you might close a coaching conversation by asking your client *So, summarise what you're taking from today's session.* Or, if you want to clarify action steps, you might say *Tell me again what you're going to do.* I sometimes find that the client is surprised when I ask them to summarise the conversation – their expectation seems to be that I as the coach will do that.

Communicating empathic understanding

This section sets out a basic formula that you may wish to use to play back to a client your empathic understanding of them and their situation. It is drawn from a chapter on communicating empathy in Gerard Egan's book, *The Skilled Helper*. Egan sets out a stylised formula that he says needs suitable modification and personalisation in practice:

> *You feel* ... [here name the correct emotion expressed by the client]
>
> *Because* ... [here indicate the correct thoughts, experiences, and behaviors that give rise to the feelings] (Egan, 2007)

He then offers some illustrations:

- You feel furious because he keeps failing to hold up his part of the bargain.
- You feel troubled because you believe that you're being left in the dark.
- You feel bad, not so much because of the pain, but because your ability to get around – your freedom – has been curtailed.

To communicate an empathic understanding, you need to recognise with some accuracy both the key emotions expressed by the client and also the crucial experiences, thoughts or behaviours that gave rise to these emotions.

In conveying your understanding of a client's emotions, you need to use the correct *family* of emotions and the right *intensity* of emotion. Egan writes that, 'The words *sad*, *mad*, *bad*, and *glad* refer to four of the main families of emotion, whereas *content*, *quite happy*, and *overjoyed* refer to different intensities within the *glad* family.'

Egan also recommends using a variety of ways to communicate your understanding of a client's feelings, and suggests four generic ways with the following examples:

- *Single word*: you're really happy
- *A phrase*: you're on cloud nine.
- *Experiential statement*: you feel you finally got what you deserve.
- *Behavioural statement*: you feel like going out and celebrating.

You may like to experiment with some of these ideas in your coaching sessions to find the kind of phrasing that you feel comfortable using and that fits with your clients. If the formula seems useful, you may also wish to consider the other aspects that Egan sets out in Chapter 5 of *The Skilled Helper*.

Taking notes

Learner coaches often ask whether it is okay to take notes during the session. My own view is that this is a matter for each coach to decide for themselves. In my own work, I always have a notepad and pen, and make very brief notes of some particular points. I tend to make notes on certain aspects of a coaching conversation. For example, if we agree a specific objective or objectives for the session, I generally write this down using the client's words. I will refer to this – perhaps in my own mind or perhaps out loud – as the session unfolds to check progress, and I am likely to review the objectives with the client at the end of the conversation.

Another time when I often make notes is when the client lists a number of points. Maybe they are listing options, or a set of criteria, or the pros and cons of a possible action. This helps me to play a summary back to the client. The physical sheet of paper with the points listed sometimes provides a visual focus for the client and me to look at together.

A third occasion when I am likely to make notes is when the client uses a word or phrase that strikes me as charged with meaning for them. Again, I will probably make reference to this as the conversation unfolds. This might take us into the realm of clean language where I try consistently to use the exact words of the client or the precise metaphor they have used. I guess that some coaches are more skilled than me at remembering the client's exact words without writing them down.

These are simply my own practices, however, and you need to decide what will suit you and your clients. There may be times when you need to, or wish to, check out with the client if they are happy for you to take notes. I have occasionally reassured the client that I will destroy the notes at the end of our session.

This leads into the question of keeping notes and records of coaching conversations, which will be considered in Chapter 7 on ethical issues in coaching.

5

Becoming a capable coach

Introduction

In *The Inner Game of Work*, Tim Gallwey writes that, 'Coaching is an art that must be learned mostly from experience'. This chapter considers how you might develop your skills and capability as a coach by, first, gaining experience through coaching real people on their real issues and, second, systematically reflecting on and learning from these experiences.

Learning from experience

In *Growing People*, I explored how managers can develop their staff by offering them fresh experiences that are challenging but achievable, and by using a coaching style of management to help them to learn from these experiences. I wrote there that:

> Deep and sustained learning – becoming able to do something you couldn't do before – only comes through experience.
> Experience on its own, however, is not enough. Experience needs to be reflected upon and made sense

of to create knowledge, and this knowledge deepens when it is applied in fresh situations. The process can be viewed as a learning cycle. (Thomson, 2006)

The learning cycle shown in Figure 5.1 is my rewording of the learning cycle set out by David Kolb in his book *Experiential Learning*.

To develop your competence as a coach, therefore, you need to progressively gain experience and to reflect upon and learn from this experience. It is as simple – and as profound – as that.

There is an analogy between learning to coach and learning to play chess. You can grasp the basic moves of chess in, say, an hour. But to become a grandmaster might take a lifetime. Similarly, in a few hours you can gain an understanding that as a coach you are trying to raise awareness and encourage responsibility, that the key skills in coaching are listening, questioning and playing back, and that the GROW model is a useful way of structuring a coaching conversation. But developing your skilfulness and resourcefulness as a coach is a lifetime journey.

| Figure 5.1 | The learning cycle |

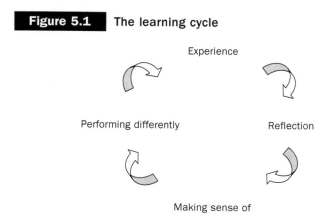

Experience

Performing differently

Reflection

Making sense of

Coaching trios

This exercise is widely used in programmes to develop coaching skills. You may wish to use it yourself, and to do so you need to find two other people who are also interested in learning how to coach. As in the silent coaching exercise described in the opening chapter, each of you has to have an issue that is real and current and matters to you, where you are central to the action, and where you are not sure how to proceed. You also need to be willing to talk about this with the two other people. I would expect that your partners will treat what you say as confidential. In the exercise, each person in the trio has the opportunity to coach, to be coached and to observe a coaching session.

Step one: 35 minutes

Agree who will be coach, client and observer first time round. The coaching session will last for 20 minutes. This will be followed by a 15-minute feedback session.

The observer acts as time-keeper. Limit the coaching session to 20 minutes – the objective is to practise and learn about coaching, not necessarily to complete the session. Indeed, if time runs out there may be valuable learning about how to manage a coaching conversation effectively.

Before the session starts it is useful for the observer to ask the coach about what areas of their practice they want feedback on. The coach might also indicate if they would like a time signal from the observer – for instance, five minutes to go.

The coach then engages in a 20-minute conversation with the client on a topic chosen by the client. The observer is silent during this (apart possibly from a time signal).

The observer then structures a 15-minute feedback session, including feedback on the areas requested at the outset by the coach. In the feedback session, avoid revisiting the content of the conversation but focus rather on the process – what did and did not go well in terms of questioning, listening, playing back, use of the GROW model, not giving solutions, and so on.

One useful way of structuring the feedback session is for the coach to begin by saying what they think they did well and what they might do differently next time. Then the client says what the coach did that was helpful and what they did that was not helpful. Finally, the observer should add anything that they have noticed that has not already been picked up in the comments of the coach or client. In this way the role of the observer is primarily to draw out learning points from the coach and client. The observer, in effect, acts as a coach, asking open questions to explore the learning points.

Step two: 35 minutes

Swap roles so that *everyone* now takes on a different role. This will ensure that each person has the chance to be coach, client and observer. Repeat step one.

Step three: 35 minutes

Swap roles and repeat step one.

Step four: 15 minutes

Individually spend some time reflecting on the three sessions and summarising personal learning points. Then share these learnings with each other. It may well be that different people have taken different things from the experience.

I put this exercise at the heart of any workshop or longer programme to develop coaching skills. For me, the exercise is a tremendously rich way of developing your coaching skills. In the space of a couple of hours you have the opportunity to engage at all four points of the learning cycle:

- to have the experience of coaching and being coached;
- to observe how someone else coaches;
- to reflect upon and make sense of three coaching sessions;
- to try out new ideas in a safe environment.

If you want to continue to develop your coaching abilities over an extended period of time, you might wish to form a trio with two others who are willing to meet with you regularly to coach and be coached.

Modifying the GROW model

The GROW mnemonic is easy to remember, so it is with a little reluctance that I introduce a modification. However, as a learner coach you may find it helpful to use the less memorable acronym TO GROW:

- Topic: What do you want to talk about?
- Objective: What would be a useful outcome from our conversation today?
- Goal: What are you trying to achieve?
- Reality: What is currently going on?
- Options: What could you do?
- Will: What will you do?

At the beginning of a coaching session, and in particular at the start of a coaching practice session in trios, it is worth establishing the topic for the conversation by asking a simple

question such as *What do you want to talk about today?*
The topic might be a vast one, far too large to be fully
covered in a single session. It is useful, therefore, to establish
an objective or outcome for this particular coaching
conversation. I also want to distinguish between the client's
goal for the session and their larger goal – that is, what they
want to achieve within the topic they are exploring.

Here is an example to illustrate the difference between
topic, objective and goal:

Coach:	What do you want to talk about today?
Client:	I'd like to explore what career I want to follow when I finish university. (A potentially large *topic*.)
Coach:	Okay. We have 20 minutes now. What would be a useful outcome for you from our time together today?
Client:	I'd like to decide whether or not to apply for jobs in the City. (The client's *objective* for the session is to make a specific decision on one aspect of their career planning.)
Coach:	Fine. Let's begin by considering what you're looking for from a career.
Client:	I really like helping people. It's important that I'm close to my roots in Inverness. And I'm not motivated by money... (Exploring the client's career *goals*.)

I find that in coaching conversations, many learner coaches
fail to establish a suitable objective for the session
sufficiently early, and so struggle to manage the conversation
effectively.

In an ongoing coaching relationship, the coach will often ask the client at the beginning for an update on what has been going on for them or on how they have fared progressing actions agreed at the previous session. As a coach, you generally need to manage the conversation so that you move onto establishing an objective for the session that is distinct from catching up on events since the last conversation. It is easy to spend too long talking about what has been happening since the last session at the expense of focusing on moving forwards.

Some of the participants on the Certificate in Coaching at the University of Warwick find it useful to modify GROW into RGOW, exploring the client's reality before addressing their goal. I would encourage you to experiment with the GROW model and find the structure that works best for you in your situation. Remember that GROW is simply one way of structuring a coaching conversation, and that raising awareness and encouraging responsibility are more fundamental ideas.

Practice clients

Another way in which you can gain experience of coaching is to find a volunteer who is willing to be coached by you over a number of sessions. You might, as an illustration, agree to have six one-hour sessions spread over six months. An arrangement like this not only gives you the opportunity to practise your coaching skills but also requires you to consider a number of ethical and practical issues – confidentiality, time and venue of meetings, note taking and keeping, and so on. Some of these issues will be explored in Chapter 7.

A practice client also gives you the chance to experience how a coaching relationship evolves over time. In the opening session you are likely to agree some form of contract with the client, which may be more or less detailed or explicit. A contract in this sense is a working agreement that clarifies assumptions and helps to manage expectations. As the relationship develops, you may find that issues arise which ought to have been considered at the outset, and hence you might learn some important points about how you will contract with future clients. As trust builds, you may find that the client is willing to share things in the third or fourth session that they held back in the opening session. You need to consider how to manage the relationship over time. One important aspect here is how to end the relationship to leave both of you, but particularly the client, with some sense of closure.

You may find it useful to spend five or ten minutes after each session making notes on the session. It may be useful to make a 'coaching review sheet' to make brief notes about the content of the session and also to capture your own learning points about your coaching practice. Such a sheet might use the following prompts:

- Name of client
- Date and venue of session
- Main topics covered
- Agreed next steps
- What did I do during the session that seemed to help?
- What did I find difficult to handle?
- What might I do differently next time?
- Any other reflections?

You can also usefully ask your practice client for feedback on how they are experiencing your coaching. You might do this on a couple of occasions – perhaps halfway through your sessions and again at the end. Questions to consider include:

- What does the coach do that helps you?
- What does the coach do that does not help you?
- What might the coach do differently?
- Any other reflections?

Ask your client to spend a few minutes capturing their thoughts and then explore these together in conversation. In listening to their feedback, resist any temptation to become defensive or to justify your actions. It is more useful simply to ask questions to clarify the feedback so that you understand more precisely what you do that the client finds helpful and less helpful. You may not agree with the client's feedback, but it is important to understand it.

Journalling

One way of reflecting on your experience is to keep a journal. A journal is not the same as a diary which records events. Rather, a journal is a place where you can record important experiences and how you thought, felt and behaved in response to what happened.

Madeline McGill writes:

> A journal is a place where we can be ourselves – where we do not have to pose – where we can remember and reflect on significant thoughts and events and so re-integrate them into the panorama of life...
>
> It is a means of talking and listening to ourselves – a way of 'speaking our thoughts' – of having a dialogue with ourselves... (Private communication)

In keeping a journal you may find that patterns emerge over time, and you understand more deeply your own motives and feelings and behaviour. For example, on re-reading your journal you might find that in a number of coaching sessions you encountered a similar situation and that on each occasion you responded in the same ineffective way. Reflecting on such a pattern might lead to learning and insight and an alternative way of responding when you next face a similar difficulty.

Supervision

If you develop your coaching skills to the point where you regularly engage in coaching conversations, you need to consider whether to have a supervisor. There is widespread agreement in the coaching literature that appropriate supervision is essential for coaches.

Peter Bluckert offers the following definition of coaching supervision:

> Supervision sessions are a place for the coach to reflect on the work they are undertaking, with another more experienced coach. It has the dual purpose of supporting the continued learning and development of the coach, as well as giving a degree of protection to the person being coached. (Quoted in Hawkins and Smith, 2006)

This definition views supervision as a one-to-one relationship, and in many ways this is the ideal. However, practical considerations of time, money and the availability of a suitable supervisor mean that other arrangements might be necessary. In group supervision, where a group of coaches meet with a supervisor, there is the benefit of sharing experiences with one another. On the other hand, in group supervision individual attention may be less than in one-to-one supervision. Another possibility, which might be a more realistic option for someone learning to coach, is to set up a co-supervision arrangement with one or two other coaches so that you supervise each other, working as a pair or as a trio. You can obviously combine different modes of supervision – for instance, in some executive coaching firms coaches have a personal supervisor and also engage in group supervision.

In his chapter on coaching supervision in *Excellence in Coaching*, Peter Hawkins writes that:

> In workshops you can learn models and develop competencies, but these do not by themselves produce an excellent coach. Supervision provides the reflective container for the trainee to turn his or her competencies into capabilities and to develop his or her personal and coaching capacities. (Hawkins, 2006)

While having a supervisor is generally acknowledged to be essential good practice for anyone coaching regularly, in fact many coaches do not have a supervisor. In 2006, a Chartered Institute of Personnel Development report, *Coaching Supervision: Maximising the Potential of Coaching*, found that, 'While 86% of coaches responding to our survey believe that coaches should have supervision, only 44% actually do so'. The report concluded that supervision is 'the pivotal link between theory and coaching practice'.

If you are in a role where you commission external coaches to work one-to-one with managers in your organisation, a key area to assess the quality of prospective coaches is to ask what arrangements they have in place for supervision. A reputable coach or coaching organisation will have well-established and robust supervision arrangements.

Coaching qualifications

In 1988, I began to work full-time in the area of management development at the British Gas National Management Centre near Stratford upon Avon. The following year I began a two-year part-time MA in Management Learning at the University of Lancaster. This gave me a foundation for my practice in management development that I'm still using 20 years later.

I was also fortunate in 1998 to be a participant on the first coaching programme offered by the School of Coaching. There Myles Downey and Jane Meyler helped me to extend what I knew about management development and counselling into an approach to coaching that has strongly influenced this book.

I am, then, a fan of investing in a sound underpinning framework to inform your practice. If you wish to develop as a coach, it is worth thinking seriously about taking a qualification. I don't mean to get a badge that you can quote when tendering for business, although this is one benefit of taking a qualification. Rather, I mean that taking time to listen, read, discuss and argue – and to practise and reflect on your practice – provides you with the opportunity to consider different models and frameworks and to work out for yourself what is the foundation of your own approach.

I am not familiar enough with the various qualifications that are currently available to recommend some rather than others. However, if you are thinking of taking a qualification in coaching, you might like to bear in mind the following questions:

- What is the time commitment?
- What is the cost, including additional travel or accommodation costs?
- Where will the programme be held?
- How long has the programme been running?
- How much experience of coaching clients do the individuals facilitating the programme have?
- How much opportunity – indeed requirement – is there in the programme to engage in actually coaching other people (both fellow participants and practice clients)?
- What are the arrangements for assessment?

Some of these questions are intended to help you think about practical matters while others ask you to consider the likely quality of the learning experience that you will encounter.

Going round the learning cycle

I don't believe that you will learn to coach effectively just by reading this book. Rather, you will learn to coach by coaching. However, I hope that the book offers you various ideas about how you might engage at the four points of the learning cycle. Figure 5.2 offers some ideas of how you could do this. I encourage you to spend time coaching, reflecting upon your coaching, refining your own approach and style, and trying out new ideas in your coaching practice.

Figure 5.2 A coaching learning cycle

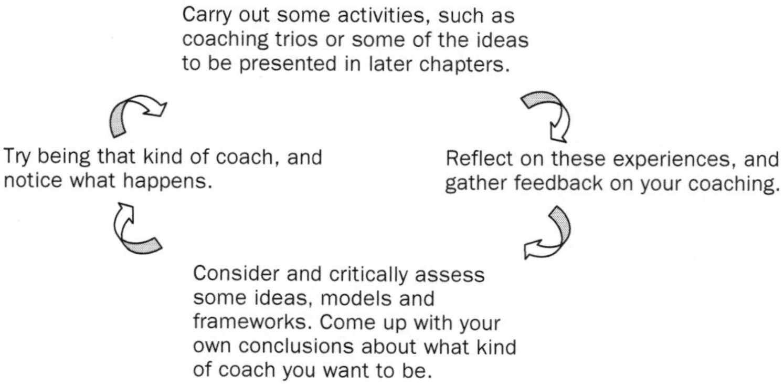

Carry out some activities, such as
coaching trios or some of the ideas
to be presented in later chapters.

Try being that kind of coach, and
notice what happens.

Reflect on these experiences, and
gather feedback on your coaching.

Consider and critically assess
some ideas, models and
frameworks. Come up with your
own conclusions about what kind
of coach you want to be.

6

Directive and non-directive coaching

Introduction

I received some feedback from one of the participants on the Certificate in Coaching that I run at the University of Warwick. She told me that I was rather directive about the importance of being non-directive. I saw straight away what she meant, and I think her feedback is accurate. In a similar way, this book is directive about the merits of the coach being non-directive. I feel somewhat like PG Wodehouse when he said that, 'I always advise people never to give advice'.

One of my aims on the Certificate in Coaching is to help the participants to think deeply about their approach in order to work out the style of coaching that best suits them in their situation. For example, another participant began to question the approach he adopted at work. He is fairly directive with his clients and although he finds that this is generally successful, he asks himself whether this actually counts as coaching. In his role he works with young people who are out of work, helping them to find a training place or a job. In addition to being unemployed, his clients often have other significant problems such as drug addiction, homelessness or low self-esteem. The nature of his role is that he sees clients for 40-minute sessions, and he is expected to meet challenging targets to ensure that a sizeable number of his clients take up a job or training place. He believes that he is unable to work non-directively as he does not have the time, and many of his clients lack the personal resources to enable him to so.

The present chapter has been informed by these conversations and other discussions with the participants on the Certificate in Coaching. With this in mind, I would like to return to something we touched on in the opening chapter, specifically, to consider where you operate as a coach on the directive to non-directive spectrum.

The directive to non-directive spectrum

Table 6.1 is based on some dimensions of one-to-one helping set out by David Clutterbuck and David Megginson in their book *Making Coaching Work*. These dimensions illustrate some of the key differences between operating at the directive and non-directive ends of the spectrum.

Table 6.1 Dimensions of directive and non-directive coaching

Directive	Non-directive
Organisation or coach sets predetermined agenda	Client has choice, with open agenda
Processes determined by coach – one size fits all	Processes selected with reference to client's preferences
Atomistic – focus on particular aspects	Holistic – relationship explores all aspects of work and life
Attend to coach's experience, or organisation norms, standards and values	Attend to client's experience, vision and values
Advice and recommendation from coach on actions	Client responsible for deciding actions

In order to coach at the non-directive end of the spectrum, you need to give primacy to the client's agenda and their view of the world, leaving responsibility for deciding what to do with the client. To check where you are on the spectrum, a really useful question to ask yourself is *Whose agenda am I following?* For instance, if you are a manager and your agenda is to accomplish one of your own objectives, or a higher-level business objective, then be clear that you are operating towards the directive end of the spectrum. Or, if you are an external coach who is working with an individual on an agenda set by the individual's organisation, then again you are towards the directive end. It may be that you employ the skills of non-directive coaching, such as listening empathically and asking open questions, to help the client decide what to do. But ultimately, if you are following an agenda set by someone other than the client, then you are to a greater or lesser extent directing them.

A related question to ask yourself when coaching and when deciding what to say or do next is *What is my intent?* If you want the client to buy into an idea of yours or to follow your advice – or if you want to steer them down a particular course more subtly – then again you are towards the directive end. Asking leading questions, or open questions with your own answer as the 'right' response, may look superficially like coaching but it isn't. Remember that to coach non-directively, you need to ask the question without any attachment to the answer.

Giving advice, making suggestions and offering feedback

Giving advice, making suggestions and offering feedback are all in varying degrees ways of working towards the directive end of the spectrum. From time to time I find that I am tempted to make suggestions or to offer solutions. There are a couple of typical situations when I may catch myself doing this. One is when I think that time is limited and I am pushing to enable the client to leave with an answer to their problem. This happened recently when a client whom I see from time to time and who is an extremely capable person came to talk through a problem with just 20 minutes till she had to leave for another appointment. Although we could easily have scheduled another meeting, I found myself making suggestions about how she might proceed. Reflecting on this afterwards, I realised that I had done this in an attempt to give the client something practical to take forward. There was no need for me to do this. In 20 minutes I could have helped her to explore the situation, to consider how she wanted to proceed, and to have reached a point where either she was clear what she wanted to do next or we agreed to meet for another coaching session. I felt very dissatisfied with how I had handled this particular meeting, so I e-mailed her the next day to ask if she would like to have a further conversation. She did, and we had a longer session where I helped her to think through the situation and to work out what she wanted to do to address it.

This client was capable. However, another situation when I occasionally catch myself offering suggestions or solutions is when I regard the client in some way as less competent. I sometimes realise that I have done this several times with a particular client. I then wonder if I am in some sense interacting as a parent – perhaps a nurturing parent – and regarding the client as being in some type of child ego-state. I therefore need to consider what is going on that makes me behave in this way with this individual when my usual style is to operate in an adult:adult way, being predominantly non-directive and leaving the client to work out their own way forward. (Chapter 11, on the psychological bases of coaching, contains an explanation of parent, adult and child ego-states.)

Hence, two situations where I find myself tempted to make suggestions are, first, when I reckon that time is limited and, second, where I in some sense regard the client as less capable.

In *Effective Coaching*, Myles Downey considers how a coach might give advice, make a suggestion or offer feedback to a client. He offers some guidelines (which, of course, read like advice!):

- First, ask the client if they would like your advice, suggestion or feedback at the moment.

- Second, if the client agrees, then say what you wish to say, which is moving to the directive end of the spectrum.

- Third, move immediately back to the non-directive end, resume coaching, and let the client choose how to respond in the light of your advice, suggestion or feedback.

You may find that when you offer a suggestion you are tempted to develop or justify it. Expanding on a suggestion you have just made may be appropriate but it does mean that you are remaining towards the directive end of the spectrum, perhaps pushing the merits of your idea. To move to the non-directive end, simply let the client respond, possibly by asking an open question such as *What do you see as the pros and cons of this idea?* Note that a question such as *What are the benefits of this idea?* may still be leading the client, unless it is followed by an equivalent question such as *What are the costs of this idea?*

The skilled helper

In *The Skilled Helper*, Gerard Egan sets out a three-stage model for the helping process:

- Stage I – The current picture: *What's going on?*
- Stage II – The preferred picture: *What do I need or want?*
- Stage III – The way forward: *How do I get what I need or want?*

Note that *I* in these questions refers to the client.

These stages are about planning for change. Egan emphasises that, for change to occur, the client needs to translate their plans from Stage III into action. There are obvious similarities between Egan's model and the GROW model described in the opening chapter. Egan also makes the point that, 'In practice the stages overlap and interact with one another as clients struggle to manage problems and develop opportunities'.

In the book – which is a classic textbook for people preparing for a career in professional helping – Egan has just two references to advice giving. In Stage I, when the helper is working to understand empathically the client's position, Egan states categorically that, 'Advice giving at this stage is out of order'. However, at a later stage in the process, the helper may wish to challenge the client's thinking or behaviour. Egan writes:

> Don't tell clients what to do. Don't try to take over their lives. Let clients make their own decisions. All these imperatives flow from the values of respect and empowerment. Does this mean, however, that suggestions and recommendations are forbidden? Of course not ... Effective helpers can provide suggestions, recommendations and even directives without robbing clients of their autonomy or integrity. (Egan, 2007)

Egan goes on to say that the client may not necessarily take suggestions, advice or directives literally but rather that ideas offered may stimulate the client to come up with their own ideas. He concludes by warning that 'helpers must proceed with caution. Suggestions, advice and directives are not for novices. It takes a great deal of experience with clients and a great deal of savvy to know when they might work.'

Egan also argues that:

> Helpers need to become radically client-centered. Client-centered helping means that the needs of the client, not the models and methods of the helper, constitute the starting point and guide for helping. Therefore, flexibility is essential. In the end, helping is about solutions, results, outcomes, and impact rather than process. (Egan, 2007)

In deciding where to operate along the spectrum from directive to non-directive, the needs of the client act as a guide for the coach.

Advice on giving advice

In a short article in the July 2007 issue of *Personal Success*, the magazine of the Coaching Academy, Lesley Matile considers whether coaches should give advice. In her view, non-directive coaching is the purest form of coaching and in this 'there is no room for advice giving'. She warns that:

> We need to remember that we are not the client. There are often huge differences – gender, age, experience, background, faith, to name but a few. Our advice is often from a different context, different culture, is historical and reflects our preferences. (Matile, 2007)

The article prompted a response from Rey A. Carr in the January 2008 issue. In an article called 'How coaches can give advice', he argues that getting advice is often the primary reason why people seek out coaches and mentors. He then describes a five-point method that he uses within a coaching session:

1. Determine the degree of risk associated with giving advice. For instance, if the client is depressed, on the one hand, or highly excited, on the other, then any advice is unlikely to be heard or acted upon, so there is no point in offering it. Moreover, if the client has little sense of a vision of what they want to achieve, then they are unlikely to understand the advice. On the other hand, people who are clear about their goals are more likely to hear advice as a suggestion rather than a command.

2. If the client seems in a suitable state to hear advice, then ask them if they would find it helpful to hear a suggestion of what you yourself did in a similar situation and how it worked out.

3. Draw upon your own experience and offer the advice within a frame of *here's what I did when I was in a similar situation.*

4. Invite the client to consider how the advice might fit their own situation, or might be suitably modified.

5. Listen to the reaction of the client and ask questions to help them to work out what to do or think.

In his third step, it is interesting that Carr offers the client advice drawn from his own experience of being in a similar situation. I guess that other coaches might offer advice based more generally on what they think will be helpful to the client but not necessarily drawn from direct experience of a being in a comparable situation.

Carr concludes by stating that:

> Advice giving is neither good nor bad in a coaching relationship. Instead, it's more useful to think of giving advice as having risks. As coaches we can reduce the risk and ensure that giving advice contributes to an empowering relationship. (Carr, 2008)

Providing information

In their book *The Counselling Approach to Careers Guidance*, two experienced careers advisers, Lynda Ali and Barbara Graham, set out an approach to help clients develop a clearer understanding of themselves and the wider issues affecting their career choices. Their approach is partly based on Egan's three-stage model described previously. One way in which careers work differs from most other forms of counselling is that careers advisers have a lot of information that may be relevant and useful to the client. An important skill for a careers adviser is knowing how to provide information effectively.

Ali and Graham state four principles of providing information:

- check out what the client already knows;
- be accurate;
- be brief – individuals can only absorb a certain amount at a time;
- always respond to a request for information – if the timing seems inappropriate, this may take the form of saying that you will come back to this later.

An important part of the skill in providing information effectively is knowing when best to offer it. Ali and Graham point out two occasions when it is appropriate to limit the provision of information. The first is when the adviser senses that the client is using a request for information to avoid facing their emotions. The second is when the adviser is tempted to escape into information-giving because the adviser themself is having difficulty with what is happening. This temptation, they write, 'is particularly strong under pressure of time, or pressure of client panic'.

Just as Egan warns against giving advice in the early stage of a helping relationship while the helper is still seeking to understand empathically the client's world, so too Ali and Graham caution against providing information too early in the conversation. They write that:

> providing information ... offers the adviser such a high level of influence. What is selected and how the information is given will significantly influence how the interview proceeds. Although information could in fact be given at any stage of the interview, its power and influence may be so great that it should ... be used sparingly and at the later stages of the exchange, once the developmental issues have been explored and clarified. (Ali and Graham, 1996)

Advice and solutions from a line manager

In Chapter 9, on coaching as a line manager, we consider a number of issues that arise when the person who is coaching is also the line manager of the individual being coached. For instance, we look at David Hemery's idea of the coaching dance, where an effective manager moves gracefully and skilfully from *telling*, on the one hand, to *listening and questioning*, on the other.

Many managers find it very difficult to operate from the non-directive end of the spectrum. Their progression to a management position, especially a senior management role, may have in large part been due to their ability to take control, to make decisions, and to get people to do what they tell them. They are accustomed to directing people, and may believe strongly that it is their role to do so. Moreover, the person being managed may expect that the manager will tell them what to do or at least give them advice. Some managers do not even realise that it is possible to manage others without necessarily being directive.

Even a manager who realises that they have a choice in how directive or non-directive to be will at times have good reasons for being directive. The manager's own performance and perhaps their remuneration may depend on the performance of the individual. Often the manager has more experience and knows exactly how they would carry out a task efficiently and effectively. They are inevitably balancing the needs of the organisation, their own objectives and the aspirations of the individual. They may also be balancing the long-term development of the individual who is learning how to do something with short-term pressures to deliver results.

There are however downsides to a management style which is overly directive. In *Fierce Conversations*, Susan Scott considers what decisions and actions a manager can delegate. Appropriate delegation taps into the ideas of others, helps to motivate them, fosters their learning and development, and frees time for the manager to do other things. In contrast, if all the important ideas and solutions, no matter how brilliant they are, come from the manager, then staff switch off and avoid taking risks. This can be incredibly expensive, she argues. She adds that, 'If your employees believe their job is to do what you tell them, you're sunk'.

Coaching versus mentoring

There are many different definitions of coaching and of mentoring. In the opening chapter we noted that it was important to define your terms, and proposed the following definitions of coaching and mentoring:

> Coaching occurs through a series of conversations in which one person uses their ability to listen, to ask questions and to play back what they have heard to create a relationship of rapport and trust that enables the other to clarify what matters to them and to work out what to do to achieve their aspirations.

> Mentoring occurs through a series of conversations in which one person draws on their experience, expertise and knowledge to advise and guide a less experienced person in order to enhance their performance or support their development.

In terms of these definitions, coaching is at the non-directive end of the spectrum while mentoring is more towards the directive end.

There are mentoring schemes in a wide variety of settings with a range of different purposes. For example, there are mentoring schemes which aim to:

- support anti-bullying policies in schools;
- help long-term unemployed people to find work;
- enable graduates to become professionally qualified;
- develop the careers of high-flying executives;
- enable women or black and minority ethnic staff to break through glass ceilings.

In some of these schemes it may be entirely appropriate for the mentor to operate at the directive end of the spectrum. For instance, it may be that the mentor has a regulatory or quality assurance role, ensuring that the client has reached certain standards before they are eligible for professional accreditation. A less capable mentor may too readily think that the best thing – perhaps the only thing – to do is to give information, advice and suggestions. However, a more skilful mentor might well spend considerable time at the non-directive end, judiciously adding advice or guidance. A mentor can be more helpful if, as well as possessing relevant experience and knowledge, they also have the flexibility to operate at the non-directive end. For example, as Gerard Egan and also Lynda Ali and Barbara Graham point out, offering advice or providing information at an early stage in a conversation is likely to be unhelpful and to significantly influence the direction of the session. Rather, a skilful mentor will in the early stages listen with empathy as the client sets out how they see the world.

Are awareness and responsibility enough?

At the end of the opening chapter we noted John Whitmore's view that you can summarise what you are trying to do in coaching non-directively using the equation:

Awareness + Responsibility = Performance

We also mentioned Whitmore's notion that awareness without responsibility is just whingeing. I have quoted this dozens of times in workshops, and it usually not only gets a laugh but makes people pause and think. I have been challenged on only two occasions, and reflecting on these challenges has led me to conclude that there is something missing from the equation. Sometimes a client is both aware of what they need to do and also keen to take responsibility to make things happen, but somehow a lack of confidence stops them from taking action. Questions of confidence, self-belief and willpower may well prevent a client who is aware and who would like to take responsibility from actually performing.

The question of ability comes in too. With your coaching, I might put in the work required to run a mile with a personal best time of, say, seven minutes. And this might be high performance for me in my situation. But all the coaching in the world won't enable me at my age and with my physique to run a mile in under four minutes.

It may be, therefore, that we need to modify the equation to read:

Awareness + Responsibility + Confidence + Ability = Performance

It follows that the agenda for a successful coaching assignment may also need to address, on the one hand, deep-seated questions of self-confidence and, on the other, issues of skill and ability levels. A training approach, perhaps involving work toward the directive end of the spectrum, might be required to develop particular skills and abilities as part of an overall development intervention.

Some evidence

In Chapter 12, on the foundations of a non-directive approach, we shall look at the ideas of Carl Rogers, the founder of a person-centred approach to therapy, counselling and education. For me, Rogers' ideas provide one of the foundation stones of my practice as a coach. In the *Carl Rogers Reader*, his biographer, Howard Kirschenbaum, and Valerie Land Henderson present a selection of Rogers' work. 'The directive versus the nondirective approach' is an extract from *Counselling and Psychotherapy*, a book that Rogers wrote in 1942. It presents the results of an unpublished thesis which analysed 19 recorded counselling interviews. A group of 'expert judges' classified counsellor responses and also rated each interview according to its directiveness. Although the sample was small and the evidence is from a long time ago, the results are startling and suggestive.

Here are some of the significant contrasts between the two approaches. Note that most of the counsellors who were rated as highly directive 'did not believe that they took the lead in the interviewing'.

- The directive counsellors did far more of the talking. Analysis of the word count showed that the directive counsellors talked nearly three times as much as the client. In the non-directive interviews the counsellors talked less than half as much as the client. So, 'the directive counselors used on the average almost six times as many words as the nondirective'.

- The techniques used by the counsellors varied. The directive counsellors employed 'techniques such as persuading the client, pointing out problems needing correction, interpreting test results, and asking specific questions'. Their approach was 'characterized by many highly specific questions to which specific answers are expected, and by information and explanation given by the counselor'.

- The non-directive counsellors used techniques such as 'recognizing and interpreting the client's verbally expressed feelings or his feeling as expressed in actions'. Their approach was 'characterized by a preponderance of client activity, the client doing most of the talking about his problems'.

Rogers goes on to suggest a crude way of assessing a recorded interview. If you read alternate items only, you will find that sometimes you can understand the trend of the interview simply by reading the counsellor's words – this indicates a directive session. Sometimes you can get a general picture just by reading the client items – this would be a non-directive session. Sometimes, of course, you just get confusion and miss the gist of the interview.

I quote this evidence not because it is conclusive but rather because it vividly illustrates some likely differences between directive and non-directive coaching conversations. In particular, it suggests that a directive coach is likely to speak far more in a session than a non-directive coach. You may find it useful to monitor this in your own coaching sessions, perhaps by considering questions such as:

- How much of the talking do you do compared with the client?

- With which clients do you speak more than you usually do? What might be the reasons for this?

- At what particular points in your coaching conversations do you tend to say more?

7

Ethical and other issues in coaching

Introduction

This chapter explores a number of ethical issues that as a responsible coach you need to think through and to work out where you personally stand. As Allard de Jong writes in a chapter on ethics in *Excellence in Coaching*, 'At the end of the day, only you can ensure your integrity in your moment of choice'.

The EMCC code of ethics

The European Mentoring & Coaching Council (EMCC) 'exists to promote good practice and the expectation of good practice in mentoring and coaching across Europe' (see *www .emccouncil.org*). Their ethical code (which it is possible to download from their website) sets out what a client can expect from a coach and hence forms the starting point of a coaching contract. The EMCC code states that, 'It is the primary responsibility of the coach/mentor to provide the best possible service to the client and to act in such a way as to cause no harm to any client or sponsor'. The code covers five areas:

- competence;
- context;

- boundary management;
- integrity;
- professionalism.

A code of ethics

I have adapted the EMCC code to produce a code of ethics for an internal coaching scheme that I set up within the University of Warwick. Under the scheme, some members of staff act as coaches to other members of staff for whom they do not have line management responsibility. The code can be summarised as follows:

- Participation – of both clients and coaches – is voluntary. Either party may break off the relationship if they feel it is not working. Both parties share responsibility for the smooth winding down and proper ending of their relationship.

- Coaching is a confidential activity in which both parties have a duty of care towards each other. The coach will only disclose information when explicitly agreed with the client or when the coach believes there is a serious danger to the client or others if the information is withheld.

- The coach's role is to respond in a non-judgmental and primarily non-directive manner to the client's performance and development needs. The aim is to help the client to articulate and achieve goals. The coach will not impose their own agenda, nor will they intrude into areas that the client wishes to keep off-limits.

- Both parties will respect each other's time and other responsibilities, ensuring they do not impose beyond what is reasonable. Both parties will also respect the position of third parties.

- The coach will be aware of and operate within the limits of their experience and expertise.
- The coach and client will be honest with each other about how the coaching relationship is working.

There are a number of points from this code that I'd like to emphasise as they are relevant to ethical coaching issues more generally. The first concerns confidentiality. For me, confidentiality is very important, though not absolute. I can envisage two ways in which I might break confidentiality, neither of which has arisen for me in practice. The first would be if I thought the client was doing something illegal. The second would be if I thought that the client might harm themselves or put themselves or others in danger. I might also discuss what has taken place in coaching conversations with my supervisor.

The second area to highlight concerns boundaries. It is essential that the coach operates within the boundary of their competence. Coaching is not therapy. In Chapter 11, on the psychological bases of coaching, we look at some psychological models underpinning different approaches to coaching. While a coach might use an exercise taken from a psychological model (for example, the parent – adult – child model from transactional analysis) it is vital that the coach stays within the boundary of their own training and experience. In a chapter on ethics in *The Reflecting Glass*, Beverly Brooks writes that, 'A strong coach, in my view, is one who "knows what he or she doesn't know" and has a strong enough ego to admit it'.

Another aspect of boundary management concerns the context within which the coaching is taking place.

For instance, in an internal work-based coaching arrangement, such as in the University of Warwick coaching scheme, it is not appropriate for the conversations to explore marital issues in any depth. The coach needs to be clear about what areas are beyond the scope of the coaching, and to manage conversations to stay within appropriate limits.

In managing boundaries of competence or appropriateness, the coach may need to refer the client to someone who is suitably qualified and experienced. It may be that the client needs to talk to a counsellor or therapist. Or they may need specialist support to develop their knowledge of business topics such as strategy or finance, or help in how to present an image of gravitas to senior people.

A final point that I would emphasise from the code relates to the voluntary nature of the client's participation. I am sometimes asked by a manager or HR professional to coach a member of staff. In my view the individual must, at some level, want to engage in the coaching. They may be anxious about coming, or they may be doubtful that the coaching will make a difference – these are legitimate worries. But, they need to be in some way open to the possibility of change and to be willing to share some of what is important to them. In practical terms, I generally ask for the client to contact me to arrange the first appointment – this requirement places some sense of ownership on them.

Two-way contracting

Some of these ethical issues can be addressed in the initial contracting between the coach and the client. The coach needs to explain to the client the basis on which they work, perhaps also sharing some relevant information to demonstrate their capability and experience. This is one aspect of checking out the 'personal chemistry' between coach and client. A contracting conversation might also cover questions of:

- frequency, length and venue of meetings;
- length of the coaching relationship;
- how to review how the coaching is working;
- severing the relationship if it is not working satisfactorily;
- how the effectiveness of the coaching will be evaluated.

Allard de Jong writes that:

> Coaches are responsible for ensuring that coachees are fully informed of the coaching contract, terms and conditions, prior to or at the initial session. These matters include confidentiality and the cost and frequency of sessions. It is your responsibility to generate a frank discussion around what this potential coachee may or may not expect and respond to her requests for information about the methods, techniques and ways is which the coaching process will be conducted. This should be done both prior to contract agreement and during the full term of the contract. (de Jong, 2006)

Three-way contracting: who is the client?

It may be that a third party has initiated coaching for someone. For instance, an organisation may arrange external coaching for one of its executives. Or, a line manager or HR professional might set up internal coaching for an employee of the organisation. In this case, there are three parties involved – the coach, the client and the individual or organisation setting up the coaching.

The EMCC code uses the term *sponsor* to refer to the organisation that commissions the coaching and the term *client* to refer to the individual being coached. The expectations and needs of the client may not be the same as those of the sponsor. For me, a guiding principle for the coach here is clarity – being absolutely clear in your own mind about what you expect, and being absolutely clear in your conversations with both the sponsor and the client.

In my own work I act as a coach within an organisation, and I am paid a salary as an employee rather than a fee for coaching. My personal stance is that my prime duty is to the person being coached – the client. I assure them in an opening contracting conversation that anything they tell me is confidential unless we explicitly agree otherwise or if I think they may do something illegal or dangerous. The client sets the agenda. However, I may have been briefed by the client's line manager or by their HR contact about the background that has prompted the request for coaching. If there are issues that the sponsor wishes to be addressed, I ask the sponsor to give direct feedback to the client. The client and I can then agree an agenda which should incorporate both the expectations of the sponsor and the needs of the client. Unless there has been an explicit agreement otherwise, I don't report back to the sponsor anything other than a vague statement such as *the coaching seems to be going well*.

Contrast the approach that I use with that of the executive coaching firm, DBM. On their website they emphasise that:

> Effective coaching directly links a leader's development to the organization's strategic objectives and defined leadership competencies. We focus on developing the skills, abilities and behaviors that lead to enhanced business performance and organizational results. This

is very different, for example, from 'life' coaching, a psychological approach to realizing individual potential outside the context of organizational business objectives. (See *www.dbm.com/content.aspx?main=386&item=387*)

In the DBM approach, therefore, the needs of the sponsoring organisation appear to take preference over the agenda of the individual. DBM is a commercial organisation whose fees for coaching are paid by the sponsoring organisation. This is one important difference between the context in which I work and in which a DBM coach works. Let me emphasise that I am not saying that one stance is better than another. Rather, I want to highlight the importance of being clear about whose expectations take priority. In practice, an experienced executive coach will often be able to balance both the requirements of the sponsoring organisation and the goals of the individual.

Beverly Brooks (2001) considers this question of whether the coach is responsible to the sponsor or the client. She too recommends clear contracting between the three parties at the outset, and adds that, 'In my experience the sophisticated buyer [of coaching services] will usually insist that the coaching objectives are shared ("the what"), but not expect that the meat of the individual sessions will be ("the how")'.

In a commercial arrangement, the question of payment arises. It is generally preferable for this conversation to be between the coach and someone from the sponsoring organisation other than the person being coached. Negotiation of fees, or resolving problems of late payment, can cloud the relationship and are best dealt with outside coaching sessions if possible. (Of course, this, is not possible if you are coaching an individual who is paying for the coaching themself.)

Evaluation

As coaching continues to grow in popularity, questions to evaluate its effectiveness will increasingly be asked, particularly by those funding the coaching. In a chapter entitled 'Evaluating development coaching' in *The Reflecting Glass*, Glenn Whitney notes that, 'Although development coaching is increasingly enjoying widespread acceptance, it will be progressively more challenged by its clients to *prove* its added value'.

The outcomes of a coaching relationship can be far and wide-reaching. Years later, the client may find that they have an insight that has its roots in a coaching conversation much earlier. These things cannot be measured and it is impossible to quantify their monetary value.

In the June 2007 edition of *The HR Director*, Gil Schwenk writes that, 'I believe trying to establish a rock solid quantitative ROI [return on investment] for coaching is a rogue argument that will tie HR departments in knots as calculations will often be based on qualitative feedback and spurious assumptions'. This reminds me of some words of Albert Einstein: 'Not everything that can be counted counts, and not everything that counts can be counted'.

However, you can gather feedback – from the client or their manager or organisational sponsor – to describe in qualitative terms what the client has gained and the benefits to their organisation. You may also be able to compare this with the objectives agreed in the contracting phase at the start of the coaching relationship, although it may be that the client has learnt things through the coaching experience that they didn't envisage at the outset. Gathering such feedback can paint a picture of how successful the coaching has been. I think this is realistic, though it may disappoint those who seek a precise financial measure.

I once arranged for a coach from The Oxford Group to work with a senior manager at the University of Warwick. He found the coaching tremendously useful. I was very impressed by how The Oxford Group assessed the effectiveness of the coaching assignment and fed this back to me as the 'sponsor'. A consultant from The Oxford Group – not the person who had carried out the coaching – conducted telephone interviews with the coach and the client. They asked two types of question – some to gather scores or ratings to measure satisfaction and others to gather verbal responses to capture the spirit of the coaching relationship. The interviewer also telephoned me to seek my sense of how the coaching had gone. They reported back a summary that covered areas such as the client's satisfaction with progress made, the level of challenge from the coach, and how well the coach had structured the coaching. The report did not reveal any content from the coaching conversations, and so did not in any way compromise confidentiality. This type of evaluation provides useful information for the sponsoring organisation, on the one hand, and the coach and their firm, on the other.

As you develop your own coaching practice, you need to consider how you will assess your effectiveness as a coach and the benefits your coaching brings to your clients and their sponsors.

Keeping notes and records

In Chapter 4 we looked at the question of taking notes during a session. You also need to decide how you will operate in keeping records of coaching conversations. Moreover, it may be that you are working in a context or in an organisation where there are rules about record keeping that you need to follow.

The website of the Association for Coaching contains their code of ethics and good practice which 'sets out the essential elements of sound ethical practice'. One element of the code states that:

> Coaches are required to maintain appropriate records of their work with Clients, ensuring that any such records are accurate and that reasonable security precautions are taken to protect against third-party disclosure. Attention must be given to the client's rights under any current legislation, e.g. data protection act. (See *www.associationforcoaching.com/about/about 02.htm*)

There are a number of reasons why you might wish to keep a record of your work with clients:

- to detail what has been agreed at the initial contracting session;
- to note in particular the client's or the sponsoring organisation's objectives for the coaching assignment;
- to record actions that the client intends to carry out so that these can be reviewed in a later session;
- to keep track of issues that are emerging through the coaching sessions and of progress over time;
- to note what your intuition tells you might be going on or to speculate about possible factors that might be important but have not been explored;
- to keep in mind what goals have been achieved and what goals are still outstanding;
- to evaluate the effectiveness of the coaching;
- to protect yourself if in some way the coaching goes wrong and you are required to account for what you have done.

In keeping records you need to consider whether there are any issues arising from any data protection legislation (such as the UK Data Protection Act 1998). I asked one leading firm of executive coaches what their practice was in this regard. They recognise that the Data Protection Act talks about 'sensitive personal data' and that to record this requires the person's permission. Sensitive personal data can include all sorts of things, including mental state. Hence, in their engagement letter to clients at the start of each coaching assignment, they refer to the Data Protection Act and sensitive personal data, and inform clients that they assume that they can keep notes to assist the coaching unless the client tells them otherwise. They also mention the possibility that the notes could be used in a supervision discussion. They ask clients to sign a short note confirming their terms of business, which includes a statement on the Data Protection Act. They are also very careful about what they do in fact record. In their experience, this issue rarely creates a problem in practice.

Having listed these sound reasons for keeping records, I have to admit that I generally don't keep records of sessions. I take each session as a fresh encounter, asking the client what they want to cover today. I assume that the client will bring up anything that is important to them. I realise that my practice in this regard might seem sloppy, and it does not follow the Association for Coaching's code, but I find that it is fit for purpose.

One thing that I sometimes do at the end of a session is to invite the client to make notes on key points that have arisen for them or on what they intend to do following the session. The notes are for them to keep, and my hope is that they will find them a useful aide memoire. After a session, I sometimes also ask clients to send me an e-mail with some bullet points pertinent to what we have been working on.

For example, after our initial session I might ask a client to summarise what they see as the objectives of our coaching work together.

Supervision

In Chapter 5 we looked at the benefits of a coach having regular supervision. Effective supervision works in the interests of the coach, the client and the sponsoring organisation. If you are working as a coach, you need to consider what arrangements for supervision will be appropriate for you.

In *Business Coaching*, Peter Shaw and Robin Linnecar write that, 'A key factor in ensuring high-quality coaching is rigorous professional supervision. This must not be skimped. Quality professional supervision is crucial for any good coach to be really effective.' They go on to add that, 'When buying coaching, the purchaser should satisfy itself that the coaching organization has effective supervision arrangements'.

In her chapter in *The Reflecting Glass*, Beverly Brooks goes further when she says that, 'I think it naïve at best, and dangerous at worst, if the coaching is not supervised by another professional with some psychological expertise'.

Finding a suitable supervisor who is located reasonably conveniently for you and whose charges you can afford might be difficult. If you are unable to find a suitable supervisor, you may wish to consider setting up a co-supervision arrangement with another coach, or setting up a regular supervision trio with two other coaches (similar to the coaching trio discussed in Chapter 5).

8

Tools you might use in coaching

Introduction

This chapter looks at a number of tools you might use during a coaching session – or perhaps in advance of a coaching conversation – to help the client become more aware of their situation or their aspirations. The tools considered are by no means an exhaustive or definitive list. Rather, I want to share some of the tools that I use in my coaching practice. The chapter will look in turn at:

- rich pictures;
- sorting cards;
- writing a letter;
- the empty chair;
- psychometric tools;
- 360-degree feedback.

Rich pictures

A technique that I use frequently is to invite the client to draw some kind of picture to illustrate their thinking or their situation. I often use the term *rich picture* to convey the notion that the picture they draw might contain a wealth of valuable information.

The most powerful experience I ever had of the potential of drawing was as a participant in a workshop where we had been asked to draw a picture representing the key aspects of our daily life. We then paired up to talk through our pictures with another. The woman I partnered pointed to an image like that in Figure 8.1.

I asked a very open question about what her picture meant to her. She was silent for some time, and it was clear that something profound was going on for her. I waited. Eventually she said *My husband is coming between me and the kids*. Through her drawing she'd seen something she had never realised before. I never met her again, and I have no idea what she did with her insight, but it was obviously deeply meaningful for her.

When I ask someone to draw a picture I always say that artistic skill is not important in this exercise – matchstick people are fine – to reassure people who may be anxious because they can't draw well. I also generally add one ground rule for the exercise – they are not allowed to use any words. However, if someone says they really are

Figure 8.1 A picture

struggling to express themself without words then I don't insist on this. Usually people draw a series of images rather than just one picture.

Asking a client to draw a picture potentially achieves a number of things. First, they necessarily have to think about their situation or their aspirations in order to represent their views as images. Second, drawing a picture often encourages the client to think laterally and to become aware of ideas – perhaps from their subconscious – that they might not have done had I simply asked them to produce a list. Third, the choice of what content to bring to the picture is left entirely up to the client. In terms of content, this is at the non-directive end of the spectrum. I am, of course, being directive in terms of structuring the session, and I am certainly attempting to focus their attention.

I sometimes leave the client on their own for five or ten minutes to do their drawing, and at other times I stay with them. However, I find it is generally more useful if they produce their picture without talking as they draw.

We noted in Chapter 3, on questioning, that it is important to choose your words carefully when asking a question. A crisp question – simply expressed – helps to focus the client's thinking. Similarly, it is important to phrase the theme of the rich picture crisply. *Draw a picture that represents your life today* has a very different focus from *Draw a picture of what you'd like to be doing in five years' time.*

There are a number of ways in which you might modify the exercise. For instance, you might ask someone to design their coat of arms, perhaps with a personal motto in any language underneath (using words for the motto!) You can leave it at that, or you might indicate that the coat of arms has to have four quarters, each representing a different theme. There are all sorts of possibilities here – as an illustration, the quarters might represent:

- what I enjoy at work;
- what life is like outside work;
- what I hope for in the future;
- how I hold myself back.

A picture illustrating the client's answers to these four questions has the potential to contain a lot of information. Going on to explore the images in conversation will often help the client to think more deeply, or spot patterns or connections, or to realise something they had been unaware of. It may produce a metaphor that, as we shall consider in Chapter 10, on metaphor and clean language, may be a rich source of insight for the client.

Another exercise that I use regularly is to ask the client to draw a line, of any shape whatsoever, to represent their life to date. I ask them to mark on the line the significant events in their life, and to make notes on how they felt or how they made decisions at key points (words are permitted!) I then invite them to talk through their life line, which can often be a powerful experience. This gives me as a coach an understanding of the client, their background, and what is important to them, and I might use this understanding to ask helpful questions. More importantly, the exercise may help clients to understand themselves more deeply.

Sorting cards

Another tool that you might employ is to ask the client to sort a set of cards. I'd like to illustrate this with an exercise that I use with people who are thinking about where to go next in their career. This uses a set of 35 cards, each representing a value that might be important to someone at work. For instance, four of the value cards state:

- VARIETY: You enjoy having lots of different things to do.
- CREATIVITY: Thinking up new ideas and ways of doing things is important to you.
- MONEY: Earning a large amount of money is important to you.
- CONTACT WITH PEOPLE: You enjoy having a lot of contact with people.

The full set of cards can be purchased via the website of their authors, Lifeskills Associates, at *www.lifeskillsintl.co.uk.*

The client sorts the cards into five categories of importance, ranging from very important to not important, according to how important it is to have this value reflected in the work that they do. The client may create their own extra cards if there are important work values for them not represented in the cards. They then rank their very important work values in order of descending importance.

The use of the cards has a number of advantages. First, the cards offer ideas for the client to consider, in a non-directive way, such as how important money is to them. Second, the client can move the cards around easily, amending their preferences as they think things through. The cards can thus be used more flexibly than a checklist. And third, the cards give a tangible representation that can help the client to focus on particular aspects of their value set.

Once the client has sorted the cards and ranked their most important work values, you can then ask open questions to help them to explore what is and isn't important to them in paid work, to consider how well their current role suits their preferences, and to explore what changes they might make to satisfy more of the work values that are important to them.

Note that the example of work value cards is simply one illustration of the more general use of card sorting to help the client become more aware of what matters to them.

Writing a letter

Another simple but potentially powerful technique is to ask your client to write a letter. As an illustration, here is an exercise I might use when the client wants to explore where they are going in the future. I ask them to pick a point in the medium or long term – for instance, in five years' time or their 50th birthday or the day they retire. I also ask them to choose someone who is, or was, significant in their life. They then write a letter to this significant person, dated at this future point. The theme of the letter is what they achieved and are proud of between today and the date of the letter. The letter is thus about aspirations for the future rather than past achievements.

I find that the exercise is generally richer when the client writes prose rather than just bullet points. I usually leave them on their own for five or ten minutes to write the letter and then ask them to read it out. We then explore what is significant for them in what they have written. Ideally, the writing of the letter should raise their awareness of what they want to do. We might then move on to work on setting goals and making action plans to achieve these.

You can make up your own theme for a letter or other piece of writing that will help a client to think things through. You could, for example, ask the client to write their own obituary as it might appear in a newspaper, or to compose the epitaph they would like to appear on their tombstone. You do, of course, need to be sensitive when asking a client to consider at some level their own death.

The empty chair

The empty chair exercise is frequently used in approaches to counselling or therapy such as Gestalt or psychodrama. I sometimes use the exercise when the client is speaking a lot during our conversation about someone who is not present in the room. For example, they may be talking at length about their manager or a difficult member of staff, or a friend who has let them down, or a figure from their past who has a large influence on their current behaviour or thinking.

To set up the exercise, you simply need to place an empty chair near the client. Ask the client to imagine that the person they have been speaking about is sitting opposite them in the empty chair. Invite the client to speak 'directly' to the other person, saying the things that matter or need to be said. Correct them if they start talking to you – it is important that they speak directly to 'the person' in the empty chair. Depending on what the client says, you might encourage them to speak further to develop certain themes.

Alternatively, you might ask the client to sit in the empty chair and to talk as if they were the other person. Inviting the client to sit in the chair of the other and look at the situation from that different perspective often helps the client to deepen their understanding of what is going on and what they need to do.

You may wish to ask the client to swap chairs a number of times, in a sense encouraging a conversation between the client and the other person.

I occasionally ask the client who has been engaged in such a conversation to stand up and then to look down and comment with a degree of detachment on what they see going on between these two people (one of whom is themself, of course). Or, I might simply ask them to reflect on what they found significant in the conversation, perhaps then moving into what they will do as a result of any insights they have had.

Although the empty chair exercise is used in psychotherapeutic settings, it is important as a coach that you are clear about how you are using the exercise and that you do not stray beyond boundaries of competence or appropriateness.

Psychometric tools

Another approach to develop a client's self-awareness is the use of psychometric tools. These range from simple questionnaires that you can download free from the internet to well-researched instruments that you need to purchase and perhaps be qualified to use.

To illustrate the use of a psychometric tool, let's look at the most widely used personality questionnaire in the world, the Myers-Briggs Type Indicator (MBTI). The MBTI was developed by Katharine Briggs and her daughter, Isabel Briggs Myers, based on the psychological theories of Carl Jung. The questionnaire is a self-report instrument, that is, respondents answer a number of questions about themselves. The underlying model proposes that each of us has an innate preference on each of four dimensions of personality. Table 8.1 shows an extract from the book *Introduction to Type* by Isabel Myers which summarises these four dimensions.

This leads to a four-letter description of an individual's personality type – for instance, INTP or ENFJ. There are 16

Table 8.1   Dimensions of the Myers-Briggs Type Indicator

Extraversion (E)	Introversion (I)
People who prefer extraversion like to focus on the outer world of people and activity	People who prefer introversion like to focus on their own inner world of ideas and experiences
Sensing (S) People who prefer sensing like to take in information that is real and tangible – what is actually happening	Intuition (N) People who prefer intuition like to take in information by seeing the big picture, focusing on the relationships and connections between facts
Thinking (T) People who prefer to use thinking in decision-making like to look at the logical consequences of a choice or action	Feeling (F) People who prefer to use feeling in decision-making like to consider what is important to them and to others involved
Judging (J) People who use their judging process in the outer world like to live in a planned, orderly way, seeking to regulate and manage their lives	Perceiving (P) People who prefer to use their perceiving process in the outer world like to live in a flexible, spontaneous way, seeking to experience and understand life, rather than control it

Source: Myers, I. (2000) *Introduction to Type* (6th edn, English European Version), Oxford: OPP.

possible combinations, and the way in which the different dimensions of the MBTI combine is significant.

Note that you need to be qualified to use the MBTI. You can find out about training workshops to become qualified from the website of the business psychology consultancy OPP (*www.opp.eu.com*).

In my own one-to-one coaching I sometimes introduce the concept of one of the dimensions, and then explore with the client how this fits with their own sense of self. For example, let's consider the extravert–introvert dimension. One way of summarising this is that extraverts speak first and, maybe, think later, while introverts think first and, maybe, speak later. Let's suppose that I am working with a client who finds it difficult to speak up in meetings. Introducing the concept of extravert–introvert may help them to understand how they behave and offer them ways of managing their behaviour. They might, for instance, decide to experiment by deliberately saying something early in a meeting and noting what happens. In Chapter 11, on the psychological bases of coaching, we look at cognitive-behavioural approaches. This example is an illustration of introducing a concept to influence the client's thinking and behaviour.

One can explore a variety of situations using the MBTI. For example, it can help in exploring issues of communication, looking at ways of persuading and influencing different people, and understanding how the individual members of a team behave and interact with one another.

I have touched on the MBTI simply as an illustration of one of the psychometric tools used by coaches. In their book *Business Coaching*, two experienced executive coaches, Peter Shaw and Robin Linnecar offer the following suggestion to anyone looking to employ a coach: 'An important question to ask a coaching organization or coach is where do psychometric assessments fit into their coaching approach. Beware of either too heavy a reliance on psychometrics or an ignorance of their use and value.'

360-degree feedback

A potentially valuable tool in coaching is the use of 360-degree feedback. It is called 360-degree feedback because the feedback is given by people from all around the individual – their manager, their peers, people managed by the individual, and perhaps customers or suppliers. The person usually also assesses themself.

There are two main ways in which 360-degree feedback can be gathered. One is via a questionnaire, completed electronically or in paper form and returned to a central point. The other way is to collect the feedback via a series of conversations, either face-to-face or perhaps by telephone.

I have constructed a number of 360-degree questionnaires on leadership and management style and behaviour. I use an external organisation, AM Azure Consulting, as the central point which sends out the instructions via e-mail, collects the responses via the internet, and compiles the feedback report. I then share the feedback with the client in a two-hour face-to-face coaching session which, first, helps the client to digest the feedback and, second, invites them to create an action plan to address what they see as the key issues arising from their feedback. (AM Azure Consulting can be contacted via their website: *www.amazure consulting.com.*)

The 360-degree report I currently use contains a mixture of numerical ratings and verbatim but anonymous comments. The numerical ratings are based on how strongly respondents agree or disagree with a number of statements about the client, such as:

- builds a collective sense of purpose, with clear and demanding performance goals;

- directly tackles issues of under-performance in ways that are both timely and effective;

- creates highly-effective working relationships with a wide range of people, particularly those in senior positions;

- shows courage and tenacity to overcome obstacles and criticism.

The verbatim comments are the responses to two questions about the individual's leadership:

- In terms of how they lead people, what do you think they are particularly good at?
- In terms of how they lead people, what could they do more effectively?

It is often the case that the client finds these textual comments more illuminating than the numerical ratings. The ratings, apart from their own and their manager's assessment, are aggregated to a certain extent so that individual responses cannot be identified. The textual comments are reported as written, but are not identified to individual respondents. Clients find it irresistible to speculate on who wrote what.

Peter Shaw and Robin Linnecar argue that oral feedback, gathered by the coach through interviews, is more effective than questionnaire-based feedback. Face-to-face interviews are in turn more effective than telephone interviews, but time and cost may rule out face-to-face interviewing. They write that, in their experience, oral feedback gathered by the coach 'is the most powerful device for getting to the bottom of important issues that need to be resolved'.

360-degree feedback can also be used to assess progress made by a client or to evaluate the effectiveness of the coaching. Feedback might, for instance, be gathered at the outset of coaching and at the end or six months later. It is important to realise, however, that information collected in this way is inevitably subjective and imprecise as a measure.

In *The Reflecting Glass*, Lucy West and Mike Milan write that although initial data-gathering through psychometrics, 360-degree feedback or shadowing of the client by the coach can be very informative, it needs to be done with caution. It can, they suggest, get in the way of developing the relationship and can 'place the locus of evaluation externally and not enough within the executive' (that is, the person being coached). Clients sometimes consider that a psychometric report or 360-degree feedback carries an authority or precision that is more important than their own considered view. Feedback needs to be digested rather than swallowed whole.

In *The Coach's Coach*, Alison Hardingham points out that all diagnostics, including psychometric tools and 360-degree feedback, need interpreting. By this she is talking about 'the work that allows a recipient of feedback to work out what it all means for him. Only when that work has been done can there be a possibility of an increase in self-awareness.'

I hope you find that some of the tools described above help you in your coaching conversations. You may already have tools that you find useful, and you will probably come across others as you develop your coaching practice. Tools like these are not a substitute for the basic coaching skills of listening, questioning and playing back. Rather the skills and the tools complement one another, enabling you to create meaningful conversations that help your clients to become more aware and to respond more effectively as a result of their increased awareness.

9

Coaching as a line manager

Introduction

This chapter looks at some of the issues that you need to consider if you are a line manager who wants to use coaching as a key aspect of the way in which you manage other people. We begin by considering some of the similarities and then the differences between coaching as a manager and coaching where you do not have direct managerial responsibility for the individual.

Similarities

The fundamental skills you need to coach as a line manager are the same as those that you need as an external coach or as an internal off-line coach within an organisation. We covered these in the opening chapters of the book. First and foremost, you need to be able to listen with good attention and with empathy to understand how the world looks from the perspective of the other person. Second, you need to ask crisp, open questions that help them to think clearly. Third, you need to be able to play back what you have heard to check understanding and to help the individual to clarify or deepen their thinking.

As a manager, you have a relationship with each of the people who work for you, and this relationship evolves through a series of conversations. You may hardly have spoken to one of your team for years – that in itself defines the type of relationship you have with that person. Coaching, similarly, is a relationship based on conversations.

In the opening chapter we looked at the equation:

$$\text{Awareness} + \text{Responsibility} = \text{Performance}$$

In later chapters we shall consider a second equation:

$$\text{Performance} = \text{Potential} - \text{Interference}$$

Both of these equations apply to the manager-coach as well as to the external or off-line coach. As a manager or a coach, you are trying to raise awareness, encourage responsibility, minimise interference, release potential and enhance performance.

Finally, as a line manager you can use a framework such as the GROW model to structure your coaching conversations.

Differences

There are, however, differences. In my book *Growing People*, I noted that in some ways it is more difficult for a line manager to coach than it is for an external coach:

> If you are a manager who wants to use a coaching approach, you have in many ways a tougher job than someone from outside the organisation working as an executive coach. You have a direct interest in the results delivered by your staff. Your performance may be measured in part by their performance, and you may have strong views on how things should be done. It can

be a real challenge to let go of control and use a coaching style to empower your people. On the other hand, while the executive coach is keen for the client to succeed, they do not have the same responsibility for performance as a manager has. (Thomson, 2006)

Another issue that poses a greater challenge for the manager-coach than for the external coach concerns confidentiality. Again in *Growing People* I wrote that:

Organisations are political institutions in which people earn a living. Even if someone has a sound working relationship with a manager, they will probably and quite wisely put limits on how open and honest they will be. An honest admission of weakness might count against someone next time there is a promotion opportunity. Individuals will usually be more open and honest with a confidant who is outside the organisation. (Thomson, 2006)

As a manager-coach you are balancing these two roles of manager and coach. It may be more useful to say that you are synthesising these two roles, for they are not necessarily in conflict. As a line manager, you are responsible for delivering results – in part through other people – on behalf of your organisation. You also, in my view, have some responsibility for developing the capability of the people who work for you, both in their interest and in the interest of the organisation. As a coach, to adapt the definition of coaching used in the opening chapter, you are seeking to enable the individual to clarify what matters to them and to help them to work out what to do to achieve their aspirations. A vital area to consider, therefore, is the degree of fit between what matters to the individual, on the one hand, and the objectives of the organisation, on the other.

When the concerns or aspirations of one of your people do not fit well with the objectives of the organisation, then it is important that as a line manager you are clear about your intentions when you sit down to converse with the individual. There are times when you need to tell the individual what the goals are, what the deadlines are, and what standards of quality are required. You are in *tell* mode. And there are times when you can genuinely explore with the individual what they would like to achieve through a piece of work, how they would like to carry it out, and when they can complete it. You are in *ask* mode.

The coaching dance

David Hemery, who won the gold medal in the 400 metres hurdles in the 1968 Olympics and who has helped many managers learn how to coach, uses the notion of a *coaching dance* to describe how a manager can move from *tell* to *ask*, and back again. As a simple illustration of the coaching dance, a manager needs to be clear when they are telling (*I must have the report by Friday*) and when they are asking (*What might you do in order to finish this by Friday?*).

The challenge to a manager-coach is to know which situations call for which approach, and to be able to move skilfully from one mode to the other. The coaching dance is summarised in Table 9.1. It contrasts a *manager-centred* approach where the manager is *pushing* the performer for results and a *performer-centred* approach where the manager is seeking to *pull* results from the performer.

On the left-hand side, the manager sets goals and targets, and gives these to the individual. On the right-hand side, the

Table 9.1   The coaching dance (after David Hemery)

The coaching dance		
Manager centred (Pushing) (Telling)		Performer centred (Pulling) (Asking)
Set by the manager	Goals and targets	Discuss and agree with performer
Reward and punish Encourage	Motivation	Ask what interests performer Performer challenges self
Pass judgments Praise and criticise Give feedback to performer	Feedback	Draw out performer's experience Help performer to generate feedback
Tell what went well and what didn't Show how it could have been done Give information	Learning	From self-awareness By reflection and discovery

manager and the individual together discuss and agree goals and targets.

On the left-hand side, the manager uses a variety of carrots and sticks to motivate the performer. On the right-hand side, the manager asks the individual what will motivate or interest them and, if appropriate, seeks to build this into the task.

On the left-hand side, the manager gives feedback. On the right-hand side, the manager helps the individual to generate their own feedback before, if necessary, adding their own comments.

On the left-hand side, the manager states how they think the task could have been done better. On the right-hand side, the manager invites the individual to reflect upon what they have learnt.

The nature of a manager-centred conversation and a performer-centred conversation will thus be very different, and very different working relationships will be created as a consequence.

Coaching in the hurly burly

It is one thing to practise coaching in 20-minute conversations with fellow participants on a workshop and quite another to use it in the hustle and bustle of day-to-day management. In saying this I don't simply mean that a manager learning new coaching skills needs time and lots of application to become fluent in using these skills. Rather, I mean that the day-to-day demands of managing in modern organisations place considerable pressure on everyone's time. And the world's problems don't come wrapped neatly in 20-minute chunks. How do you as a busy line manager embrace a coaching approach when you are perhaps already working longer hours than you would like? Here are a few ideas.

There are occasions in organisational life which are well suited to adopting a coaching approach, for example, when a manager and an individual sit down formally to carry out a performance and development review. This should be an occasion where time is consciously set aside for a conversation to take place. This conversation lends itself readily to a coaching approach where the manager can ask open questions to help the individual to reflect on their strengths and weaknesses, their successes and challenges, their hopes and aspirations, their goals and objectives. Panel 9.1 offers a set of open coaching questions from which you might select a subset to structure a performance and development review.

Panel 9.1 Performance and development reviews

You can design a performance and review process around a series of open coaching-type questions that structure and record a conversation between a manager and an individual who works for them. Having a meaningful conversation is far more important than the paperwork.

A useful review document is one that is live and that is regularly in the thoughts of the individual. It is not a piece of paper that is filed in a drawer to be extracted 12 months later when it is time for the next round of reviews.

Here is a list of questions from which you can choose a subset to structure a meaningful review process. There are three sets of questions – to review performance, to set objectives and to create a development plan. The questions are worded to put the individual at the heart of the process.

- How well did you achieve your objectives over the last 12 months?
- What successes and disappointments did you have?
- What did you learn over the last year?
- What are your key objectives for the coming year? (Note that agreed objectives may need to take account of higher-level business objectives.)
- What help or support do you need to achieve your performance objectives?
- What deadlines or milestones will you set?
- When – and how – will you monitor progress in achieving these objectives?
- What are your strengths, both technically and behaviourally?
- What are your limitations, both technically and behaviourally?
- What are your aspirations for the future?
- What development goals do you want to set yourself?
- What specifically will you do to achieve these goals?

This assumes that the individual is willing to take part in such a conversation. You can't coach someone who does not want to be coached. If such conversations have never taken place before in the organisation, or if you as a manager never engage in adult-to-adult conversation with your people, then the individual may well be suspicious of your motives and be very guarded in what they choose to reveal. If, on the other hand, the climate within your team or organisation is one where reasonably open and honest discussion is normal, then such reviews provide an ideal opportunity to use a coaching approach.

When I run workshops to help managers to develop their coaching skills, one question that regularly arises is *How do I coach my boss?* Invariably, when I ask the individual why they want to coach their boss, the answer is that they want to get their boss to agree to something. This isn't coaching! It may be influencing or persuading or manipulating, but it is not coaching. You can test this simply by asking *Whose agenda are you following?* or *What is your intention?* You can coach your boss only if you are on their agenda – and if they are willing to engage.

Another occasion where time may be available and where a coaching approach is particularly appropriate is at the start of a new piece of work or project. And if in your team or organisation projects are explicitly reviewed – while in progress or on completion – you have a further opportunity to use coaching, particularly in order to share feedback and to capture learning points.

In case you have the impression that coaching can only take place in extended conversations, note the view of John Whitmore that any single question that makes the other person think is coaching. For example, he recommends asking *What would you do if I wasn't here?* He suggests that if a manager asks this question when one of their people requests their help, then it invites the other to think for themself, to become more aware and to take more responsibility. A word of caution, however. I said this once to my daughter, then aged 11, when she asked for help with her homework. She slammed the kitchen door, muttering *Oh, you're no use!*

Assuming both parties are willing, there are many situations that offer the opportunity for an impromptu coaching session. For example, if you and a colleague are travelling to a meeting together, you might use the occasion to have a coaching conversation. Short coaching-type conversations on matters that aren't confidential or sensitive can take place very informally – in the corridor, at the coffee machine or in the cafeteria queue. It may be tempting in such a situation where time is limited to offer a quick piece of advice. If you are tempted to offer advice, it is worth checking your intent before you do so.

There is another important point to make regarding the time taken to coach one of your people. To what extent do you regard the time that you spend coaching your people as a cost or as an investment? In *Growing People* I wrote that, 'If you establish a coaching style of management and avoid getting immersed in detail, then not only will your people perform and develop but you will also free your own time to think more strategically and to work fewer hours'. Here is a simple example that makes the point. Imagine that you are a parent with a four-year-old child who cannot tie his shoelaces. (The example predates the use of Velcro!) It is quicker today to tie their shoelaces for them than to help them learn. However, if you're still tying their shoelaces ten years later, then not only will you have devoted a lot of time to this, but your child will not have developed an important capability. Taking time to coach one of your team may well save you far more time than you originally invest.

Coaching a team

The topic of coaching a team probably warrants a separate book. In this section I'd simply like to make a few points relating to how a line manager might coach their team.

The key notions of coaching, reiterated in the opening paragraphs of this chapter, apply equally to coaching a team or an individual. Your basic challenges are to raise awareness and generate responsibility within the team, and you do this through your conversation and relationship with the team, using the skills of listening, questioning and playing back. You can use the GROW model to help your team to think through a challenge. It may well be easier to generate options because a number of people can build on each other's ideas. On the other hand, it is generally far more difficult for a group of people to reach a decision to which all are committed than it is for an individual to resolve to do something.

In *Growing People*, I wrote that, 'Because you are dealing with a number of people, coaching a team is more complicated than coaching an individual. There may be complex group dynamics going on within the team that affect how it operates and which might be difficult to fully understand.' This is putting it mildly! One of the challenges in coaching or managing a team is simply to be able to notice not only what is going on for each individual but also to get a sense of the various interrelationships between individuals and between different subgroups. Becoming aware of factors such as these, and working out how to respond, is several orders of magnitude more complicated than working one-to-one.

In his coaching and consultancy work, Peter Hawkins often suggests that it is far more powerful to act at the points where the parts of a system relate to one another than it is to act on the separate parts. In team coaching, this means that coaching to enhance relationships between individuals and between subgroups will be more powerful than simply coaching all of the individuals in the team. Just as a team can be more than the sum of its parts, so too coaching a team is more than coaching the individuals in the team.

A coaching culture

I believe that it is possible to do useful work as a coach or as a manager-coach even when the surrounding culture of the organisation is indifferent to the notion of coaching. However, the impact will be far less than if the organisational climate is one that supports the use of coaching. The effects of coaching in an indifferent environment are likely to be confined mainly to helping the individual recipients of the coaching and are unlikely to shift the organisation significantly. Moreover, even when an individual has benefited from coaching it will be more difficult for them to apply their learning when the attitudes and behaviours surrounding them are not supportive. Indeed the individual might respond to their heightened awareness by leaving the organisation.

Moreover, it is impossible to create a true coaching culture unless the person at the top of the organisation is firmly committed – through their actions rather than merely their words – to coaching as a way of managing and developing individuals, teams and the organisation. To move beyond the rhetoric of creating a coaching culture requires a journey of many years. In their book *Coaching, Mentoring and Organizational Consultancy: Supervision and Development,*

Peter Hawkins and Nick Smith describe seven steps that organisations need to go through to evolve a coaching culture:

1. The organisation employs coaches for some of its executives.

2. The organisation develops its own coaching and mentoring capacity.

3. The organisation actively supports coaching endeavours.

4. Coaching becomes a norm for individuals, teams and the whole organisation.

5. Coaching becomes embedded in the HR and performance management processes of the organisation.

6. Coaching becomes the predominant style of managing throughout the organisation.

7. Coaching becomes 'how we do business' with all stakeholders.

Hawkins and Smith go on to argue that it is important for the organisation to be clear about the end to which the coaching culture is the means. On the basis of over 20 years' experience of a variety of culture change initiatives, they write that, 'If the culture change endeavour becomes an end in itself, it will not be sustained beyond the energy of its enthusiastic creators.' They also say that sustaining such a long-term programme will require ongoing measurement and evaluation.

Servant-leadership

Some time ago, I was coaching a senior manager who had a particularly inclusive style of leadership and who was extremely supportive of his staff and their wellbeing and development. At the same time, he faced considerable pressure to deliver on behalf of the organisation as he led the creation of a new business unit. I introduced him to the idea of servant-leadership, and this gave him just the conceptual framework he needed to carry out his role as a leader who wanted to trust and nurture his people. In this section, I'd like to summarise the key ideas of servant-leadership briefly and to consider how they relate to a coaching style of management.

The term *servant-leadership* was first coined in 1970 by Robert Greenleaf in an essay entitled 'The servant as leader'. He wrote:

> Becoming a servant-leader begins with the natural feeling that one wants to serve, to serve first. Then conscious choice brings one to aspire to lead. That person is sharply different from one who is leader first...
>
> The difference manifests itself in the care taken by the servant first to make sure that other people's highest priority needs are being served. The best test, and most difficult to administer, is: Do those served grow as persons? Do they, while being served, become healthier, wiser, freer, more autonomous, more likely themselves to become servants? And what is the effect on the least privileged in society; will they benefit, or, at least, not be further deprived? (Greenleaf, 1970)

In his foreword to *Insights on Leadership*, a collection of essays edited by Larry Spears, Stephen Covey writes of the impact of the global economy demanding that firms produce more for less and at greater speed: 'The only way you can do that is through the empowerment of people. And the only way you get empowerment is through high-trust cultures and through an empowerment philosophy that turns bosses into servants and coaches.'

A simple illustration of servant-leadership is seen in the inverted organisation chart which puts the people who deal with the organisation's customers at the top of the chart, those who manage the customer-facing staff below, and senior management at the bottom of the chart supporting everyone else. In his chapter in *Insights on Leadership*, Kenneth Blanchard explores this idea of inverting the pyramid. He concludes by saying that servant-leadership is all about 'making goals clear and then rolling your sleeves up and doing whatever it takes to help your people win. In that situation they don't work for you – you work for them.' Blanchard also makes clear that when we talk about servant-leadership we aren't talking about a lack of direction. Servant-leadership involves both the visionary role of setting direction and the implementation role of translating the vision into reality.

Probably the best known servant-leader in public life in recent times is Nelson Mandela. Other names often mentioned as examples of servant-leaders are Mahatma Gandhi, Mother Teresa and Martin Luther King. Each of these had a clear vision and was able to enthuse followers to help them realise their vision. Equally, each had a vision that was essentially in the service of others.

The idea of the leader as servant is, of course, a metaphor. We shall look in some detail at the power of metaphors in the next chapter. The servant-leader metaphor may seem naïve and impractical to someone whose metaphor of leadership, probably unconsciously, is about command and control. Some managers with a strong need to control others find it very difficult to trust their people. The opposite of control within an organisation is not necessarily lack of control. In many ways, the opposite of control is trust. In *The Manager as Mentor*, Michael Marquardt and Peter Loan write:

> The effective manager trusts her employees and they trust her. She keeps her word, and she keeps their

confidence. She expects greatness of her employees. She has experienced the power and productivity of teams and knows she can delegate problems to her employees working in teams without doubt that they will find the best solutions. (Marquardt and Loan, 2006)

In an interview some months after the September 11 tragedy of 2001, Margaret Wheatley reflected on what to do when it is not possible to control events:

> The only way to lead when you don't have control is you lead through the power of your relationships. You can deal with the unknown only if you have enormous levels of trust, and if you're working together and bringing out the best in people. I don't know of any other model that can work in the world right now except servant-leadership. (Wheatley 2002b)

Servant-leadership, then, is about supporting people, seeking to bring out the best in them, trusting them, and dispensing with the illusion of control. It seems to me that an important part of translating the idea and ideal of servant-leadership into practice within and across organisations is through a coaching approach to management and relationships. Listening in order to understand people, and asking questions to help them clarify what matters to them and what they need to do to succeed, are ways to coach others, to lead others and to serve others. But coaching, like servant-leadership, is far more than some tools in the managerial toolkit. At its best, coaching, like servant-leadership, is a way of *being* as well as a way of managing.

10

Metaphor and clean language

Introduction

In this chapter I want to look at two ideas – metaphor and clean language – and invite you to consider how you might use or adapt these ideas in your own coaching practice. We begin with metaphor.

Metaphor

When we speak, we often use metaphors to express ourselves. A metaphor uses words in a way that is not literal. We might, for instance, say that a footballer has 'the heart of a lion'. We don't mean this literally, but rather we are trying to convey notions of strength, determination and bravery.

I expect that most readers would agree that our thoughts are in part determined by the words we use to describe things. Hence, it is a small step to say that if we speak in terms of metaphors then it follows that we also think in terms of metaphors.

Now, how we think informs how we act. If you approach me with your right hand outstretched and a smile on your face, and if I think that you are extending a friendly greeting to me, then I am likely to respond by offering my own right hand in a handshake. If, however, you approach me with your fists clenched and a scowl on your face, and if I think that you intend to attack me in some way, I will respond quite differently.

I want to suggest, therefore, that not only do we speak and think in terms of metaphors but that we also at times act on the basis of our metaphors. In other words:

- we speak in terms of metaphors;
- we think in terms of metaphors;
- we act in terms of metaphors.

In *Growing People*, I put it this way:

> As human beings, we use language to think about and talk about our world. The language we use shapes the frames through which we view the world. And how we see the world affects how we behave and the actions we take. (Thomson, 2006)

In their book *Metaphors We Live By*, George Lakoff and Mark Johnson express this more strongly. They write that, 'Metaphor is pervasive in everyday life, not just in language but in thought and action ... Our ordinary conceptual system, in terms of which we both think and act, is fundamentally metaphorical in nature.' In their view, 'Reality itself is defined by metaphor'.

Similarly, in *Images of Organisation*, Gareth Morgan writes that, 'The use of metaphor implies a way of thinking and a way of seeing that pervade how we understand our world generally'. He says that his book 'is based on a very simple premise: that all theories of organization and management are based on implicit images or metaphors that lead us to see, understand, and manage organizations in distinctive yet partial ways'. He then goes on to explore eight metaphors for making sense of organisations – for instance, the organisation as a machine, an organism or a brain. Each of these metaphors offers a partial view of organisations, suggesting notions such as raising efficiency (from the machine metaphor), adapting to a change in the business environment (from the organism metaphor) or becoming a learning organisation (from the brain metaphor).

In *Forms of Feeling: The Heart of Psychotherapy*, Robert Hobson describes his conversational model of therapy which aims to help people with significant relationship problems to disclose, explore, understand and modify these problems within an extended therapeutic conversation. He writes that, 'In psychotherapy we need to learn, and to share, the language of our patient in developing a conversation. An important activity is that of giving life to significant metaphors.'

Now, coaching isn't psychotherapy, and it is vital that as a coach you respect the boundaries of your competence and of your contract with your client. Having said this, however, you may like to consider how you might use metaphor in your work with your clients. One way in which you might do this is to encourage them to think about their situation in terms of metaphors. This has the potential to enable them, first, to understand their world somewhat differently and, second, to find possible ways forward. In other words, it has the potential both to raise awareness and to generate responsibility.

In my own experience, I sometimes find that a client uses a metaphor that seems particularly vivid or meaningful. When this happens, I encourage them to explore their metaphor further. A simple phrase such as *Say a bit more about...* is often all that needs to be said to allow them to think more deeply.

Another way in which you might use metaphor is to pull together some of what the client has said and offer a framework for thinking about their situation. I sometimes find that a metaphor occurs to me as a way of doing this, and I will then offer it tentatively to give the client the opportunity to agree with, to disagree with or to develop the metaphor. As an illustration, I was working with one client who found herself having to take a role within her organisation that was not what she really wanted to do but which enabled her to continue working there. I introduced the notion of finding a place on a lifeboat to enable her to survive until she moved to where she really wanted to be. She found this a helpful image, and brought it up again in subsequent conversations over a period of months. Then in one conversation she began to talk about being on a life raft. After she had used the term several times I pointed out that *lifeboat* had given way to *life raft*, and we explored what was different for her in being on a life raft rather than a lifeboat. One difference she identified was that a life raft seemed to her to be a craft that is drifting without a rudder.

As we shall see in the next section, there are some coaches and therapists who would strongly oppose the idea that a coach might introduce a metaphor to help the client make sense of their world. In *Time to Think*, Nancy Kline warns against paraphrasing the client's words:

> The best wording is the Thinker's own: their mind has specifically chosen and uttered those exact words for a reason. Those words mean something to the Thinker. They come from somewhere and are rich with the Thinker's history, culture, experience and any number of associations in the Thinker's life. (Kline, 1999)

This is one area where you need to think about your practice and work out your own position on rephrasing the client's words or on offering a metaphor that occurs to you as a potentially rich way of looking at the client's situation. This leads us on to the notion of clean language.

Clean language and symbolic modelling

In the 1980s, a trauma therapist called David Grove noticed that many of his clients described their symptoms using metaphors. He found that when he asked them questions using their exact words their perception of their trauma began to change. He developed the notion of *clean language* to ask questions that employ the exact words and even non-verbal expressions used by the client. Here, the language is 'clean' in that the client's words have not been modified and thus contaminated by the therapist. Grove also reckoned from his study of transcripts of famous therapists such as Carl Rogers that they shifted their client's frame of reference by rewording what the client said.

Two other therapists, Penny Tompkins and James Lawley, studied closely what Grove did and how his clients responded. (For more about their ideas, see their excellent website *www.cleanlanguage.co.uk*. The following quotes are taken from various articles on this website or from their book *Metaphors in Mind*.) They developed his ideas into an approach which they call *symbolic modelling*. They write:

> Symbolic Modelling is a method of facilitating individuals to become familiar with the organization of their metaphors so that they discover new ways of perceiving themselves and their world. It uses Clean Language to facilitate individuals to attend to their verbal and nonverbal metaphoric expressions so that

they create a model of their own symbolic mindbody perceptions. (Lawley and Tompkins, 2001)

They use clean language questions that employ the exact words and metaphors used by the client. In their view, the power and richness in the metaphors used by the client contain valuable information for the client. If the coach rewords what the client says, this introduces a different model of the world.

Not only do they use the exact words of the client, but they also ask questions in very specific ways, employing mainly a dozen basic clean language questions. For instance, using XYZ to represent some of the exact words of the client, they might ask questions such as:

- And is there anything else about XYZ?

- And where does XYZ come from?

- And what kind of XYZ is that XYZ?

According to Tompkins and Lawley, clean language has three functions:

- to acknowledge the client's experience exactly as they describe it;

- to focus the client's attention on an aspect of their perception;

- to send them on a quest for self-knowledge.

In their article, 'Less is more ... The art of clean language', Tompkins and Lawley offer the following example:

Client: I'm stuck with no way out.

Therapist 1: Have you got the determination to walk away?

> Therapist 2: What would happen if you could find a way out?
>
> Therapist 3: And what kind of stuck with no way out is that stuck with no way out?

Therapist 1 is using very unclean language, implying that the solution is for the client to be away from their current situation, that determination is the resource required, and that the client will 'walk' away (rather than, say, 'leap' away).

Therapist 2 uses cleaner language, but assumes on behalf of the client the solution to 'find a way out'. Both Therapist 1 and Therapist 2 subtly ignore the client's perception – the client said there is no way out of stuck. If the client is stuck, 'then there is valuable information in the stuckness'.

Clean language is used to 'allow information to emerge into the client's awareness by exploring *their* coding of *their* metaphor'. The aim is 'for the client to gather information about their own subjective experience, not necessarily for the therapist to understand it'.

Asking further clean language questions allows the client to develop their metaphor. For instance, the client might reply to Therapist 3's clean language question in one of the following three ways, all containing different metaphors:

> Client A: My whole body feels as if it's sinking into the ground.
>
> Client B: I can't see the way forward. It's all foggy.
>
> Client C: Every door that was opened to me is closed.

These metaphors might be explored with further clean language questions. According to Tompkins and Lawley, the client will often go on to develop other metaphors that provide the key to resolving their issues. They write that:

... symbolic resources naturally emerge which resolve, at a symbolic level, that which the client has been unable to resolve at an everyday level. *When the metaphor evolves, behaviour changes in the client's 'real world'.* There is a correlation between the two. (Tompkins and Lawley, 1997)

I find that clients vary in their willingness to work with metaphors. As mentioned above, I sometimes find that a client uses a metaphor that seems particularly significant. I may then use their exact words to invite them to explore the metaphor further. Sometimes this goes nowhere but sometimes it leads to a rich exploration of their situation, with some new insights and greater awareness.

As an example, I explored with one client a metaphor that she introduced to describe how she felt about being in conflict situations. She likened this to being attacked physically on the head. She was well aware that this described her situation metaphorically, not literally. She then identified the notion of putting on a mask – like a welder's mask – to protect herself. She considered how a mask could help her to behave effectively when in a conflict. When she tried this out in practice, she found that mentally putting on her mask did indeed enable her to behave effectively when faced with conflict situations. She took this notion further and deliberately chose her dress and makeup – her mask – at the start of each working day to ready herself for any conflict that might arise through the demands of her role.

In this illustration, my intention was to work with the client at a cognitive level, hoping that a shift in her thinking would provide the basis for a change in behaviour – and this is what seemed to happen. However, Penny Tompkins and James Lawley also use clean language and symbolic modelling to work in a psychotherapeutic way with clients. They write that:

> Some clients benefit just from having their metaphors developed with a few clean questions. For some the process leads to a reorganisation of their existing symbolic perceptions, while for others nothing short of a transformation of their entire landscape of metaphors will suffice. As a result clients report that they are more self-aware and at peace with themselves, that they have a more defined sense of their place in the world and how to enrich the lives of others. (Lawley and Tompkins, 2000)

Using metaphor and clean language in coaching

On the clean language website there are a number of articles about the use of metaphor, clean language and symbolic modelling in coaching. In her article 'Using metaphors with coaching', Angela Dunbar writes that the basic principles are congruent with any good coaching practice:

- ask questions to find out what the client wants;
- ask questions to find out what needs to happen for them to get there;
- If problems, barriers or blocks are identified, ask questions to find out what needs to happen to overcome them.

Another coach, Carol Wilson, writes in an article called 'Metaphor & symbolic modelling for coaches', that:

> The technique fits smoothly into a coaching session and is particularly effective when a client seems stuck, or

trapped in repeating behaviour patterns. By the use of metaphor, issues are tackled at a far deeper level than the conscious mind can reach, and changes in behaviour start immediately. (Wilson, 2004)

She suggests that, 'Focusing on a metaphor enables the client to communicate directly with their subconscious'. She says that, 'The process is safe, easy to learn and a joy to experience'.

This raises a note of caution for me, however. If you are considering using clean language and symbolic modelling in your coaching, you need to be clear whether or not your intention is to work 'at a far deeper level than the conscious mind can reach'. There is considerable potential in these ideas, but you need to recognise the boundaries of your competence and training, as well as the nature of your contract with your client.

In terms of the directive–non-directive spectrum that we looked at in an earlier chapter, clean language and symbolic modelling are very much at the non-directive end. I guess anyone who reckons that Carl Rogers is 'shifting the client's frame of reference' could claim to be very non-directive. But Tompkins and Lawley recognise that even a coach or therapist using clean language is nevertheless directing in some sense. In 'Metaphors in mind: A case study', they write:

> Of course Clean Language influences and directs attentions – *all* language does that. Clean Language does it 'cleanly' because it is sourced in the client's vocabulary, is consistent with the logic of their metaphors, and only introduces the universal metaphors of space, time and form. (Lawley and Tompkins, 2001)

There are echoes here of Myles Downey's comment that it is impossible to be completely non-directive because 'the slightest flicker of concern in the eye, the faintest smile of approval will show up and be read and interpreted by the player'.

More about training programmes in clean language and symbolic modelling is available on the Clean Language website (*www.cleanlanguage.co.uk*).

On the other hand, you may feel that working with clean language is not for you. Nevertheless, being conscious of the notion that there is a power in the exact language used by your client and in the metaphors they use to describe their experience will help you to listen attentively and with empathy, to phrase your questions well, and to play back more accurately what you have heard and observed.

11

Psychological bases of coaching

Introduction

The starting point of this chapter is a comment by Lucy West and Mike Milan in an appendix to their book *The Reflecting Glass*: 'There are three main schools of Western psychology – psychoanalytic, cognitive-behavioural and humanistic. Whether implicitly or explicitly, development coaches practise primarily from one of these orientations.'

In this chapter I'd like to summarise the three schools briefly and then to look in more detail at a number of particular approaches – transactional analysis, psychosynthesis and Robert Hobson's notion of a community of selves. You can use these approaches within each of the three schools of thought. As we explore the ideas, I encourage you to consider how you might adapt some of them to use in your own practice as a coach.

The three schools of Western psychology

The summaries in this section draw in part on material by a psychotherapist, Christine Webber, on the website *www.netdoctor.co.uk*. She writes there that, 'The major difference between coaching and psychotherapy is that coaching is present and future focused'.

Psychoanalysis is an intense form of talking therapy, devised a hundred years ago by Sigmund Freud and developed by others since then. All forms of psychoanalysis assume that the keys to understanding lie in the unconscious mind. You are not aware of your unconscious, but it has a huge influence over who you are and how you act. True psychoanalysis involves several sessions a week over many years, and so can only be afforded by those with lots of spare time and money.

Psychodynamic therapies, of various kinds, also assume that the feelings held in the unconscious mind are powerful and often too painful to be faced. This leads to defence mechanisms such as denial which we all deploy to protect ourselves. Psychodynamic therapies aim to help the patient to surface their true feelings so that they can experience and understand them. These approaches are generally much shorter than psychoanalysis, and will usually focus on a more specific aim such as dealing with a phobia.

Cognitive-behavioural therapy (CBT) is based on the idea that our thoughts (or cognitions) affect our moods and feelings, on the one hand, and our actions and behaviour, on the other. Negative thoughts – *I'm hopeless at that, I'm stupid, I'm not worthy, I'll never succeed* – lead to negative feelings such as unhappiness or depression, and also mean that we avoid situations or perform poorly. A CBT therapist will not delve into the unconscious origins of these feelings and fears but rather will work with the patient to help them, first, to think in more helpful ways and, second, to develop new behaviours in a step-by-step way to deal with difficult situations. A CBT therapist may help the patient to learn simple techniques such as breathing deeply to control anxiety.

In 2004, the National Institute for Clinical Excellence published a report recommending that CBT should be one of the preferred means of treatment for mild to moderate depression. CBT is also seen as one of the most effective treatments where anxiety is the main problem.

Humanistic psychology affirms the inherent value and dignity of human beings. It views people as striving to find meaning and fulfilment in their lives. It has a hopeful, constructive view of people and of their capacity to grow and to shape their own lives. Humanistic approaches emerged in the 1950s as a third force distinct from both the psychodynamic approaches and the behaviourist approaches.

A leading figure in the development of humanistic psychology was Carl Rogers, who pioneered person-centred therapy and counselling, as well as a student-centred approach to education. The next chapter will look at how Rogers' view that people are motivated to fulfil themselves can be regarded as the basis of the approach to coaching developed by, among others, Tim Gallwey, John Whitmore and Myles Downey. Whitmore reflects this when he writes that, 'Coaching is unlocking a person's potential to maximize their own performance'.

Transactional analysis

Transactional analysis – or TA as it is often called – is a psychological theory that seeks to explain how individuals think, feel, behave and interact with others, often in patterns that are repeated through life. Developed originally by Eric Berne, TA uses a number of concepts that are expressed in simple and vivid language. The ideas in TA can be considered at a number of levels, ranging from simple explanations of how people behave to a coherent framework used to effect lasting change by counsellors or therapists.

In *Transactional Analysis Counselling in Action*, Ian Stewart writes that:

> The philosophical assumptions of TA can be summed up in three statements:
>
> - People are OK.
>
> - Everyone has the capacity to think.
>
> - People decide their own destiny, and these decisions can be changed. (Stewart, 2000)

These philosophical assumptions sit comfortably with a non-directive, person-centred view of coaching, and TA might be used by someone subscribing to a humanistic view of psychology. Equally, however, you might use TA as the basis of a cognitive-behavioural approach or, with appropriate training and experience, as a psychodynamic approach.

One of the key concepts in TA is that of *ego-states*. TA describes three mental states that each of us switch between – parent, adult and child. Stewart describes the ego-state model as follows:

- At certain times the person will be behaving, thinking and feeling in ways that replay his own childhood. At such times he is said to be in a *child* ego-state.

- At other moments the person may behave, think and feel in ways he has copied in childhood from his parents or parent-figures. He is then said to be in a *parent* ego-state.

- When the person's behaviour, thoughts and feelings are neither replayed from his childhood or borrowed from parental figures, but instead are direct responses to the here-and-now, he is said to be in an *adult* ego-state.

In *I'm OK – you're OK*, Thomas Harris writes:

> Continual observation has supported the assumption that these three states exist in all people. It is as if in each person there is the same little person he was when he was three years old. There are also within him his own parents. These are recordings in the brain of actual experiences of internal and external events, the most significant of which happened during the first five years of life. There is a third state, different from these two. (Harris, 1974)

The parent-adult-child model can be used not only to explore individual behaviour but also to look at the relationships between people. A common pattern of behaviour is that a manager operates from a parent ego-state and someone who works for that manager engages with them from a child ego-state. This creates a series of parent–child transactions that sets the framework for their relationship. I have on a number of occasions introduced the model to help a client to think about a working relationship – the client might be a manager engaging with their staff in some kind of parent mode, or the client may be an individual behaving in some sense like a child in relation to a manager or authority figure. Clients generally find the model easy to grasp and it often helps them to make sense of an unsatisfactory working relationship. This might be viewed as a way of raising awareness in the client.

What, then, about encouraging responsibility? The key to breaking a pattern of parent–child transactions is for the client to operate consistently from an adult ego-state, and to continually invite the other party to operate from an adult ego-state. The intention is to replace the unhelpful pattern with a new pattern of adult–adult transactions. Note that the client has no guarantee that the other party will respond from an adult ego-state, but they do have choice in how they respond to non-adult behaviour.

I can think of a number of other situations where I have introduced the parent-adult-child model. One is when the client needs to behave more assertively with others (not necessarily with a line manager). For instance, they might recognise that they behave passively in some contexts, operating from a child ego-state. A second situation is when a manager (seeking to operate from an adult ego-state) wants to help one of their team who isn't performing well and who doesn't want to take responsibility. In this instance the poor performer may be continually acting from a child ego-state. Despite the manager's intention to stay in the adult ego-state, the child in the poor performer hooks the parent ego-state in the manager, who ends up taking more responsibility than they wish to.

Another idea from transactional analysis that you might like to explore is the notion of *life-script*. Eric Berne, the founder of TA, maintained that each of us early in childhood decides upon a plan for our life – our life-script. This is influenced by our parents and our early environment, but it is also a decision that each of us makes. The decisions we make in early childhood are not through the kind of deliberate thinking that we might use later in life. Rather, they are emotional decisions we make in response to external pressures as a way of surviving and having our needs met in a world that is often perceived by infants as hostile.

These early childhood experiences and decisions mean that we end up following a life-script such as:

- *I mustn't be me* (which might manifest itself in feelings of inferiority);

- *I mustn't be a child* (which might inhibit someone from being playful, having fun or behaving spontaneously);

- *I mustn't do anything* (which might lead to over-cautiousness and inability to make decisions).

Note that the life-script planned by the individual as an infant is not necessarily the same as their life story. What actually happens will be affected by decisions the individual makes as an adult, including decisions for change that they may make through coaching or counselling. As the examples indicate, to explore a life-script in depth with a client may mean working at a psychodynamic level and is not to be engaged in by a coach who is not competent to do so.

At a less intense level – at a cognitive level, perhaps – a coach might help a client explore and address an issue such as perfectionism in terms of having a *driver* to *be perfect*, a habitual way of behaving that has been shaped by their upbringing or childhood experiences. Five common drivers are:

- be perfect;
- be strong;
- try hard;
- please others;
- hurry up.

When a client becomes aware that their working style is based on one of these drivers, they then have greater choice over how to behave. They can utilise the strengths of their driver when this is appropriate, and they can choose to respond differently when it isn't – in other words, they needn't be ruled by their driver.

Psychosynthesis

Psychosynthesis is another approach to understanding human psychology. Developed originally by Robert Assagioli, an associate of Freud's, psychosynthesis takes the view that each personality consists of a number of elements that need to be in harmony – to be synthesised – for healthy human growth and development.

The summary of psychosynthesis below draws on information provided by the Psychosynthesis and Education Trust (*www.psychosynthesis.edu*):

> The first step in psychosynthesis is the attainment of a certain level of self-knowledge, the ability to move within one's inner world with both ease and confidence … In this work we make a surprising discovery: instead of being consistent, unchanging individuals, we find ourselves to be a mixture of contrasting, changing elements, which in psychosynthesis are termed subpersonalities. (See *www.psychosynthesis.edu*)

These subpersonalities are like the instruments that make up an orchestra. Because we tend to identify with whichever subpersonality is dominant in a particular situation, the orchestra sounds like it is tuning up – a cacophony rather than a harmonious ensemble.

The website goes on to say that:

> When we are identifying this way with one single part of ourselves, we become ruled by it, we are enslaved by an illusion … Such identification is a universal process which can be reversed only by its opposite: disidentification, an attitude whereby we consciously detach ourselves from all the various aspects of our

144

personality, thus allowing ourselves to discover our true 'I', our centre. (See *www.psychosynthesis.edu*)

This awareness of our subpersonalities and of our true centre is important but it is not enough. Lasting change also requires the discovery and use of will. In their chapter on transpersonal coaching in the book *Excellence in Coaching*, John Whitmore and Hetty Einzig write that:

> will is essential if we are going to act in the world. It provides motive force, a sense of direction and energy to make things happen. It underpins our ability to live our lives with purpose. At a pragmatic level, will is expressed through responsibility – the choice to take ownership for one's actions; then through the purposeful life and, at the highest level, a sense of being part of the purposeful universe. (Whitmore and Einzig, 2006)

A final point in this summary of psychosynthesis is the notion of the superconscious. This is the level of our unconscious where, in the words of Whitmore and Einzig, we can find 'access to our higher qualities, creativity, aspiration, inspiration, peak experience and our meaning and purpose'.

To work with a client using the full range of ideas from psychosynthesis is once again to work at a psychodynamic or psychoanalytic level, and requires an appropriate degree of training, experience and expertise. Psychosynthesis is very much based on a humanistic psychology, viewing individuals as having an inherent tendency towards synthesis and harmony. It also sees the individual as part of a bigger interconnected picture, part of a collective unconscious.

As with transactional analysis, it is possible to borrow some of these ideas and use them at a cognitive level to help clients become more aware and then perhaps to take responsibility for behaving differently. As an illustration, I was working with one client who behaved confidently and assertively in some situations but held himself back in others. I invited him to expand on how he thought, felt and acted in these contrasting situations. I then asked him to give these two versions of himself a name. When he was acting confidently and forcefully, he reckoned he was behaving like the Alexander the Great. The name that occurred to him to capture how he felt when he was behaving hesitantly was Julian. We then explored how he might deliberately bring his assertive *Alexander* self to the fore when he next found himself thinking and acting from his passive *Julian* self. There was no need to mention the term *subpersonality* at any point in the conversation. (Note that although this client chose two male names, another client might have chosen labels such as *director* and *conformist*.)

A community of selves

The concepts expressed in psychosynthesis are similar to an idea described by the psychotherapist Robert Hobson in his book *Forms of Feeling: the Heart of Psychotherapy*. He develops the notion that each of us is a community of selves. For example, we might say we are *in two minds* about something, or that we are *battling* with ourself. 'The smallest community is one of two persons.' However, there may be 'other dimly recognized, or unknown selves or sub-personalities'. Hobson writes that this 'way of elaborating experience is often valuable in self-understanding and in therapy'.

He goes on to describe how one client imagined his various 'selves' as 'a troupe of actors (the Conversationalist, the

Business man, the Country Bumpkin, the Adventurer, the Sentimental Lover, the Metropolitan Smooth Man and the Dreamer) with a vacillating and not very effective Producer'. Another client 'talked as if he was composed of a number of political factions: "hard liners", "soft liners", and a "middle-group"' with a speaker 'trying to present to the world a view of the whole "community"'. In therapy this client developed these into '"relaxed", "friendly" and "free and easy" groups', which enabled him to engage more actively with other people.

Hobson emphasises that '"self as a community" is a metaphor within which some persons can express many aspects of experience in relation to themselves and others'. He adds that, 'These separate "identities" can be more or less related or they can be divorced. There is, however, a tendency towards an harmonious organization: a whole with an integrated activity of differentiated parts.'

Some clients will be able to work easily with this notion and express themselves through this kind of metaphor, and others won't. For example, my client mentioned in the previous section found it easy to label his assertive self *Alexander the Great* and his passive self *Julian*.

There is a hierarchy within the community of selves – 'all do not have the same power of willing and acting'. The producer and the speaker in the illustrations above, for example, have some kind of executive function, trying to coordinate the different actors or factions.

Each of us needs to act from a sense of self. However, this is always partial. When we assume that this is our only possible identity we restrict our development. Hobson says that, 'Usually the maintenance of this limited self, which may be expressed in an efficient social and professional life style, often accompanied by apparent self-knowledge, conceals a chaotic non-society of other selves. That way madness lies.'

Applying these ideas in coaching

We began this chapter with a quote from Lucy West and Mike Milan that development coaches practise primarily from a psychoanalytic, cognitive-behavioural or humanistic school of psychology. It is useful to bear in mind these three views of human psychology, and to consider where you yourself stand in your own practice. The ideas summarised above from transactional analysis, psychosynthesis and a community of selves can be applied within each of the three schools of psychology.

Although the ideas might be used by a coach operating from a psychoanalytic or psychodynamic orientation, most coaches – and managers using a coaching style – are not qualified to work in this way. I am clear in my own mind that I am not qualified to use a psychoanalytic approach.

Each of the ideas might be used by a coach who takes a humanistic view that it is possible for individuals to develop, grow and shape their own life. In TA terms, people are OK. In psychosynthesis terms, we can discover our true 'I', our centre. In Robert Hobson's words, there is a tendency towards a harmonious organisation.

As illustrated briefly above, a coach might introduce a notion such as parent-adult-child or of different selves to help a client to examine their thoughts, feelings and behaviour. This is using a cognitive-behavioural approach to help the client to make sense of their world, to appreciate how they might see their world differently, and to consider what behaviour they wish to change as a consequence of this fresh perspective. You can view this as attempting, first, to raise awareness and, second, to promote responsibility.

When I started writing this chapter I considered that I operated from a primarily humanistic perspective, using a predominantly non-directive stance. In becoming aware of how frequently I introduce a concept or model to help the client to think differently, I realise that I am working more at a cognitive level than I had appreciated. In recognising that there are some models that I use regularly, I begin to question why I introduce these particular models and to what extent I might be directing the client to, at least, think along certain lines. I may not be as non-directive as I had thought.

Although the opening quote from Lucy West and Mike Milan prompted me to write this chapter, I am not sure I agree with their premise that coaches implicitly or explicitly practise primarily from one perspective. My own practice seems on reflection to be a blend of humanistic and cognitive-behavioural approaches. Interestingly, in an obituary in *The Guardian* of Robert Hobson, who died in 1999, his colleague Frank Margison writes that whenever Hobson's 'work was presented at scientific meetings, almost invariably the audience would say that his "conversational model" was no different from the model they practised – whether they were cognitive therapists, Rogerian counsellors, psychoanalytic psychotherapists or psychiatrists'.

The above summaries of TA, psychosynthesis and the community of selves are mere sketches. If the ideas are new to you and you are intrigued by some of them, you might seek to develop your knowledge and understanding to a point where you feel confident and ethically sound in adopting or adapting the ideas. There are, of course, many other psychological schools of thought you can explore and which might inform your work. I encourage you to find out more about some of these ideas and to think through how you will use or adapt them in your own coaching practice.

12

The foundations of a
non-directive approach

Introduction

This chapter sets out briefly some of the philosophical foundations that underpin a primarily non-directive approach to coaching. I hope that reflecting on the ideas of Carl Rogers and Tim Gallwey raises useful questions for you to think about as you approach the task of coaching another human being.

Carl Rogers and the person-centred approach

For me, the work of Carl Rogers and his person-centred approach to psychotherapy, counselling and teaching provide the philosophical foundations of non-directive coaching. I don't think the importance of his ideas is adequately recognised in the coaching literature.

Carl Rogers was born in 1902 and died in 1987. He is regarded as the founder of an approach to psychotherapy variously described as non-directive, client-centred or person-centred. He was one of the leading figures in the humanistic psychology movement of the 1960s, 1970s and

1980s. He wrote prolifically, and his writing style is very personal and easy to read. His writings have influenced practice in fields such as education, medicine and social work as well as psychology and therapy.

In an article published a year before he died, 'A client-centered/person-centered approach to therapy', Rogers states briefly his central hypothesis:

> It is that the individual has within himself or herself vast resources for self-understanding, for altering his or her self-concept, attitudes, and self-directed behavior – and that these resources can be tapped if only a definable climate of facilitative psychological attitudes can be provided. (Rogers, 1989b)

Later in the article he says that:

> Practice, theory, and research make it clear that the person-centered approach is built on a basic trust in the person. This is perhaps its sharpest point of difference from most of the institutions in our culture. Almost all of education, government, business, much of religion, much of family life, much of psychotherapy, is based on a distrust of the person. (Rogers, 1989b)

He goes on to add that, 'The person-centered approach, in contrast, depends on the actualizing tendency present in every living organism – the tendency to grow, to develop, to realize its full potential ... It is this directional flow that we aim to release.'

These quotes illustrate the contrast between the directive and non-directive ends of the coaching spectrum. When you sit down to coach someone, what are your own fundamental assumptions about human nature in general and the client opposite you in particular? To what extent do you trust that the client has the resources to work out for themselves what they want and how to achieve this?

Carl Rogers' three conditions for effective facilitation

In the article, Rogers describes the three conditions that he says are both necessary and sufficient to create an effective relationship that lets the other person grow, whether in the context of therapy, education, management, parenting or coaching. To provide Rogers' 'definable climate of facilitative psychological attitudes', the facilitator needs to have and to demonstrate three things to the other person:

- *congruence*: being genuine, being real, sharing feelings and attitudes, not hiding behind a façade;

- *unconditional positive regard*: non-judgmental acceptance and valuing of the other, in a total not conditional way;

- *empathy*: understanding the other's feelings and experience, and also communicating that understanding.

Note that it is important that you not only possess these qualities but also that the client to some extent perceives your congruence, unconditional positive regard and empathic understanding of them.

An important part of my own learning as a management development practitioner was taking part in the MA in Management Learning at the University of Lancaster between 1989 and 1991. When it came to writing a dissertation towards the end of the programme, I chose to look at my own practice. In one chapter I assessed myself against these three conditions of Rogers. I gathered feedback from people who had taken part in programmes that I'd run and whom I felt had seen me at close enough quarters to offer a view. Based on their feedback and on my own sense of what I did well and not so well, I rated myself in terms of congruence, unconditional positive regard and empathy. At that time, I reckoned that:

- I was naturally very good at being congruent;

- my positive regard for others was in fact highly conditional – I regarded some people very positively but made very negative judgments about others;

- I was okay at empathy but needed to work at this – some of my colleagues were naturally more empathic than me.

I found it a very useful exercise, and I have worked hard over the years to develop my ability to accept others unconditionally and to listen in order to understand both the verbal and non-verbal communications of others. You might like to spend some time considering – or gathering feedback on – your own strengths and limitations in terms of congruence, unconditional positive regard and empathy. You might do this in terms of your overall practice as a coach, or you might reflect on different coaching sessions with individual clients.

Tim Gallwey and the inner game

The ideas of Tim Gallwey have had a huge influence on the type of coaching explored in this book. For instance, in the first edition of his book *Coaching for Performance*, John Whitmore states that in Britain 'all the leading exponents of business coaching today graduated from or were profoundly influenced by the Gallwey school of coaching'. And in

Effective Coaching, Myles Downey writes that Gallwey's book *The Inner Game of Tennis*, first published in 1974, 'is perhaps one of the most influential books on performance and learning of the last thirty years'.

Tim Gallwey was an educationalist and tennis coach. A gifted tennis player himself, he describes a key moment when at the age of 15 he missed an easy volley on match point in a national championship quarter-final match. He relived this moment for many years thereafter.

Later, while coaching tennis, he observed carefully what happened in his tennis lessons. He realised that in giving lots of instruction about things like how to hold and swing the tennis racket, he was overteaching and causing confusion in his players. He concluded that in coaching tennis he 'had to learn how to teach less, so that more could be learned'.

Gallwey noticed that the players he was coaching would talk to themselves, giving themselves endless commands to keep their eye on the ball, to bend their knees, and so on. He postulated that within each player there were two selves – Self One who seems to give instructions to Self Two who carries out the actions. Self One then evaluates how well or badly Self Two has performed. He writes that 'the key to better tennis – or better anything – lies in improving the relationship between the conscious teller, Self One, and the unconscious, automatic doer, Self Two'.

In *The Inner Game of Tennis*, Gallwey contrasts the outer game, played against the opponent on the other side of the net, with the inner game 'that takes place in the mind of the player ... against such obstacles as lapses in concentration, nervousness, self-doubt and self-condemnation'. He missed that volley on match point not because of any lack of technical ability but because of the negative thoughts going through his mind.

Myles Downey describes Self One and Self Two as follows:

- Self One is the internalised voice of our parents, teachers and those in authority. Self One seeks to control Self Two and does not trust it. Self One is characterised by tension, fear, doubt and trying too hard.

- Self Two is the whole human being with all its potential and capacities including the 'hard-wired' capacity to learn. It is characterised by relaxed concentration, enjoyment and trust.

Gallwey describes the negative thoughts of Self One as interference. It is this interference that prevents the player from performing to their potential. You might summarise this in the equation:

$$Performance = Potential - Interference$$

It follows that one way to release potential and raise performance is to minimise interference – interference from lack of confidence, from trying too hard, from fear of failure, and so on. If as a coach you can help your client to reduce these inner obstacles to performance, then their natural ability will enable them to perform.

A key issue is this notion of 'natural ability'. Think for a moment about all the things your body needs to synchronise just to hit a moving tennis ball, irrespective of where it lands. It requires considerable coordination within your body. Developing this idea, Gallwey suggests:

> There is a far more natural and effective process for learning and doing almost anything than most of us realize. It is similar to the process we all used, but soon

forgot, as we learned to walk and talk. It uses the so-called unconscious mind more than the deliberate 'self-conscious mind'. (Gallwey, 1975)

Thus, in Gallwey's view, people learn best by tapping into their own natural learning processes.

One way of reducing the inner thoughts that interfere with performance is to focus attention. This can be demonstrated using a physical activity such as catching a ball, playing a tennis shot or hitting a golf ball. Here is a simple exercise that illustrates the point.

Ask for a volunteer who considers that they are not very good at catching a tennis ball. Throw the ball to them, asking them simply to tell you what they notice. They might say something like *The ball is green* or *The ball is spinning* or *There is some writing on the ball*. Continuing to throw the ball, ask them what they are most interested in. Let's assume they are interested how high the ball is when it reaches them. Ask them to tell you more about how high the ball is. They might say *It's about three feet high*. Ask them to tell you how high the next ball is, and so on.

What generally happens is that the volunteer catches most of the balls. Your questions to them, following their interest, in effect compel them to watch the ball carefully. Their natural coordination then ensures that they catch the ball. If, instead, you had given them the instruction to watch the ball carefully, it is likely that their Self One would have in various ways told their Self Two how poor they were at catching a tennis ball, and this interference would have made the prophecy self-fulfilling.

Gallwey calls the mental state required to reduce interference, the state demonstrated in this simple experiment, 'relaxed concentration'. By focusing attention, by simply noticing what is happening, the performer can enter this mental state of relaxed concentration that enables them to perform closer to their natural potential.

I would be somewhat sceptical about this had I not experienced it at first-hand on a number of occasions. I have been the performer hitting much better tennis backhands than I'd ever done before, or swinging a golf club more fluently than ever before. It really does work – find a partner and try it!

Two equations

I'd like to play with the two equations that we have looked at for performance. If the idea of playing with equations scares you, you might like to reflect on what your Self One may be saying to your Self Two.

Recall from an earlier chapter that:

Awareness + Responsibility = Performance

And, as we have seen earlier in this chapter:

Performance = Potential – Interference

It follows, therefore, that:

Awareness + Responsibility = Potential – Interference

Let us assume that, for any individual, *potential* is fixed, even though none of us comes close to fulfilling all of our potential. It follows that anything which increases *awareness* or which increases *responsibility* must decrease *interference* (which has a minus sign in the equation). In the ball-catching exercise, the increased *awareness* from focusing on the ball reduces the *interference* from negative thoughts.

On the other hand, if as a coach you can help your client to address an *interference* that is stopping them from taking action then you will at the same time increase the likelihood that they will take *responsibility* for acting. For example, you might help a client to overcome negative thoughts such as *I can't do this* or *I'll never be successful* or *I don't know how to get started*.

Rogers and Gallwey

There are obvious similarities in the views of human nature taken by both Carl Rogers and Tim Gallwey. Rogers speaks of the actualising tendency present in everyone – the tendency to realise our potential. Gallwey, meanwhile, writes of the natural process of learning that is similar to how we learned to walk and talk.

John Whitmore contrasts this humanistic model of humankind with the behaviourist view that we are 'little more than empty vessels into which everything has to be poured'. Whitmore favours the humanistic model which proposes that 'we are more like an acorn, which contains within it all the potential to be a magnificent oak tree. We need nourishment, encouragement and the light to reach toward, but the oaktreeness is already within.'

Rogers' views also underpin how I approach the design and facilitation of the various management development workshops and programmes that I run. In his book *On Becoming a Person* is a sentence that I have spent more than 20 years reflecting upon: 'It seems to me that anything that can be taught to another is relatively inconsequential, and has little or no significant influence on behavior'.

Similarly, in his more recent book *The Inner Game of Work*, Gallwey writes that 'The coach is not the problem solver. In sports, I had to learn how to teach less, so that more could be learned. The same holds true for a coach in business.' He also says that 'coaching is not so much about telling the client what *you* know as it is about helping him to discover what he already knows, or can find out for himself'.

In his article 'A client-centered/person-centered approach to therapy', Carl Rogers notes that when he is at his best as a facilitator or therapist, he is closest to his inner, intuitive self. He says at this time that his *presence* is releasing and helpful. 'There is nothing I can do to force this experience,' he writes.

This has echoes of Gallwey's 'relaxed concentration'. Similarly, Myles Downey, very much influenced by Gallwey, writes of those occasions when he is able to coach with fluency and joy from his Self Two.

In the next chapter we shall develop this idea of coaching from your inner, intuitive self and look at how you might coach at your best by mastering the inner game of coaching.

13

The inner game of coaching

Introduction

In the previous chapter we looked at some of the ideas of Tim Gallwey. In particular, we considered his notion of the *inner game* – that is, the game 'that takes place in the mind of the player … against such obstacles as lapses in concentration, nervousness, self-doubt and self-condemnation'. We noted the distinction between Self One – our internal, controlling voice that is characterised by tension, fear, doubt and trying too hard – and Self Two – the natural, learning self which has lots of potential and is characterised by relaxed concentration, enjoyment and trust. We also considered Gallwey's equation that, for the client:

Performance = Potential – Interference

This chapter explores the inner game that takes place in the mind of the coach rather than the client. What are the interferences that might limit your ability to perform to your potential when you are coaching? How can you as a coach silence your own Self One and converse gracefully and skilfully from Self Two?

Preparing for a coaching session

There are a number of things you can arrange in advance of a coaching session to make it more likely that you will start the conversation free from distractions. At a simple level, do you have everything you need to hand? Do you have a pen and a notepad, a box of tissues, an empty chair, a flipchart and pens, a cup of tea or coffee, a clock, or whatever you need to coach in the style you use? If you keep notes on your clients, have you had enough time to read these through and to think about what this might imply for the coming session? Will you be free from interruptions, such as someone knocking on the door or a phone ringing?

Think about the room in which the coaching takes place – is this ready? One consideration is whether the coaching takes place on your premises or the client's premises or on 'neutral territory' such as in a hotel. If the venue is not on your premises, what might you do to ensure that the room is set up as you wish? If the venue is the client's office – not an ideal place but sometimes that is where it is – what are the arrangements to manage interruptions? In any venue, what are the ground rules between coach and client about mobile phone calls or messages? These are some of the basic issues to think about in advance and to make suitable preparations to minimise interference before the coaching starts.

What state of mind are you in as you get ready to coach? You may, for instance, have arrived in a rush from a previous meeting, out of breath and with your mind full of what you've just been engaged in. You may be thinking about what you will be doing after the session and wondering if you are suitably prepared. Or you may have found some peace and quiet to leave behind your various concerns, to begin to focus on the client, and to still your mind.

One practice that you may find useful is to take a few minutes before each coaching session to relax. You might have your own preferred way of doing this. Here are a few ideas, some of which you may wish to use. Find a quiet place – perhaps the room in which the coaching will take place or perhaps your own car if you have driven to meet the client – and seat yourself comfortably. Close your eyes. Listen – what noises can you hear? What do you notice about your body – release any tension you feel in your neck or shoulders or forehead, or wherever. Take a slow, deep breath in. Hold that breath. And breathe out fully. Take a few more deep breaths. Release any other sources of tension that you become aware of as you breathe. Now think about the client who is due to arrive. Picture them in your mind's eye. Recall how they speak. Imagine how they might walk into the room in a few minutes' time. Focus back on yourself. Sit still for a little while, letting any thoughts that enter your mind come and then go. When you are ready, open your eyes and prepare to greet your client.

Taking some time to ground yourself in this kind of way can help you to let go of the irrelevant thoughts and concerns that are cluttering your mind.

Peter Hawkins of the Bath Consultancy Group often suggests that the times of the client's arrival and departure are those when rich unconscious material may be revealed. The client may say something very important in answer to a greeting such as *How are things?* Or they may display a piece of body language or facial expression that speaks volumes about how they are feeling or the state of mind they are in. On the way out after the session, the client may say something very important as they relax, considering that the session is over. This is sometimes referred to as the *doorknob effect* – as when, for example, an anxious and embarrassed patient raises what they are really concerned about just as they are leaving their GP's consulting room.

Interference during a coaching session

In this section I'd like to look at some of the interferences that can arise for the coach during a session with a client. In his chapter 'Training for development coaches' in *The Reflecting Glass*, Myles Downey, writes some words that go to the heart of the inner game as it applies to coaching:

> The primary function of the coach is to understand, not to solve, fix, heal, make better or be wise – to understand. The magic is that it is in that moment of understanding that the coachees themselves understand for themselves, become more aware and are then in a position to make better decisions and choices than they would have done anyway. That is how coaching is profoundly simple and simply profound. But most of us struggle to get above our own agenda and want to be seen to be making a difference. (Downey, 2001)

When coaching, I sometimes find that I start to feel some kind of responsibility for ensuring that the client solves their problem. I am, in Downey's terms, seeking to solve or fix or make better, wanting 'to be seen to be making a difference'. This is interference. It might also be viewed as my Self One telling me to try hard and make sure I do a good job. My guess is that it is an interference that is common, not least with those who are learning how to coach. It is important, when this happens, to notice it and then to remind myself that I am not responsible for coming up with solutions and that my role is to manage the relationship and the conversation in the service of the client. As Tim Gallwey says, 'The coach is not the problem solver'. Or, as Nancy Kline writes, 'Usually the brain that contains the problem also contains the solution – often the best one. When you keep that in mind, you become more effective with people. And people around you end up with better ideas.' I find that not feeling responsible for making things better is tremendously liberating, enabling me to coach more gracefully and effectively.

One way in which we may slip into fixing things for the other person is through what Kline calls *infantilisation*. She defines this as 'the act of treating someone (including children) like a child, deciding for them what is best, directing them, assuming we know better than they do, worrying about them, taking care of them'. In transactional analysis terms, the coach acting in this way is operating from a parent ego-state, seeking to control the other person and inviting a response from the client's child ego-state. Kline says that:

> You infantilize when you want the well-being of another person intensely but you also intensely want to be seen as expert, indispensable and brilliant. Infantilizing others is actually an act of profound insecurity. It looks big and confident, but it is a cover for feeling small and doubting deeply. (Kline, 1999)

Another interference that arises, not least with newcomers to coaching, is to become concerned about what to say or do next while the client is talking or thinking. John Whitmore warns that, 'if the coach is working out the next question while the coachee is speaking, the coachee will be aware that he is not really listening'. So, in this situation, there is interference both for the coach, who is thinking of the next thing to say, and for the client, who perceives that they are not being fully listened to.

Recall the simple exercise described in the previous chapter where a volunteer is asked to catch a tennis ball and is encouraged to focus on an aspect of the ball that interests them. This is an exercise to silence the interference of Self One – typically some version of *I'm hopeless at catching* – and allow the volunteer's natural ability to coordinate eyes and hands to emerge. Following interest means that the volunteer actually watches the ball very carefully. This is generally far more effective than the injunction *Keep your eyes on the ball*.

As a coach, how then do you quieten a Self One which is saying *I need to solve things* or *I must come up with a really good question*? What do you focus on that is equivalent to watching, say, the spin of the tennis ball? A powerful way to do this is just to listen with respect, interest and empathy. Simply pay attention to the client continually, seeking to appreciate their world. If you can focus on this, then you are less likely to be distracted by such Self One thoughts. As Nancy Kline says, 'The quality of your attention determines the quality of other people's thinking'.

Another source of interference may arise for an executive coach who is in a three-way contract involving themselves, the individual being coached, and the organisation that is sponsoring the coaching assignment. The sponsor may be represented by the individual who has commissioned the coaching, such as the chief executive or the HR director. In this situation, the coach may be balancing the needs of both the client and the organisation, and it may be the case that the expectations or requirements of the organisation create interference in the mind of the coach as they converse with the client. At times, the coach needs to hold these expectations at the back of their mind as they focus within the session on attending to the client. At other times, the coach may need to bring these expectations to the front of their mind and to enquire of the client how what is being discussed fits with the requirements of the organisation. In a situation such as this, clear contracting at the outset is very important.

In Chapter 3, on questioning, I raised the notion that as a coach you need to ask the question without any attachment to the answer. In choosing a question, the coach may well be inviting the client to focus on an important aspect of their situation. We need to be prepared to hear and accept an answer that surprises us and reminds us that our understanding of the client's world is inevitably and always partial. Similarly, if we use an exercise such as inviting the client to draw a picture or asking them to speak to the empty chair, we need to introduce the exercise without any attachment to the outcome.

One of the things that can happen in a coaching session or relationship is that the words, feelings or gestures of the client stimulate in the coach a memory of their own situation or past experience. It may even be that something in the unconscious of the client triggers something in the unconscious of the coach. In psychological terms, this is known as *countertransference*. These unresolved aspects of the coach's life – their baggage or unfinished business – can be another source of interference, getting in the way of coaching effectively.

Myles Downey discusses this kind of interference in a short article called 'The inner game' in The School of Coaching alumni newsletter of February 2007. He sometimes recognises that he is saying to himself *I am not good enough*, which he regards as useless and as a vestige of his upbringing. One of the factors that Downey sees as improving his own inner game as a coach – which also enhances the inner game of his clients – is that he has a 'brilliant psychotherapist'. It is obviously not practical for every coach to have their own therapist, and many coaches will be able to coach well enough without psychotherapy. But Downey's comments remind us, first of all, that our own psychological baggage can get in the way of our coaching well and, second, of the importance of supervision in the professional development of coaches.

In *Coaching, Mentoring and Organizational Consultancy: Supervision and Development*, Peter Hawkins and Nick Smith describe an interference which they call the 'deference threshold'. This might manifest itself in the coach losing the plot, feeling small or feeling like they are on the back foot. The coach defers to the client, and feels disempowered. This may be particularly the case for an inexperienced coach, but it can afflict even very experienced coaches. This is akin to the soccer team at the top of the league having a dreadful game for no apparent reason. Hawkins and Smith say that the deference threshold 'is not a precise feeling' but involves the coach handing 'over their authority, presence and impact to the other person'. Somehow the coach sees themself in 'the role of the outsider, who does not have a legitimate reason for being there'. A vital part of managing yourself as a coach is to notice when your deference threshold has been triggered – 'awareness is the key', say Hawkins and Smith. They also recommend that the coach discuss these times with their supervisor.

You might like to reflect on your own coaching and identify the interferences that get in the way of you coaching well.

Potential and Self Two

Let's look now at the inner game of the coach in terms of how they can bring more of their potential to their coaching conversations and how they can use their natural, learning Self Two.

We noted above that Self Two is characterised by relaxed concentration, enjoyment and trust. An analogy with driving a car may illustrate what relaxed concentration might feel like. As a learner, we do not expect to be able to drive a car after a couple of lessons – it takes time, practice and experience. A novice driver has to concentrate hard on individual aspects, such as steering, braking or changing gear. An experienced driver does these things apparently without thinking, and may arrive at their destination with little memory of the journey. However, there are times when the experienced driver has to respond intelligently and quickly to deal with a tricky situation on the road.

In a similar way, we coach best when we can bring a relaxed concentration to it. We are aware of things happening at a number of levels as we process various types of information. We are continually deciding what to do next, but this does not feel burdensome. There are also times which seem particularly significant, where we need to consider carefully the next step in the coaching session.

In the final chapter of *Effective Coaching*, Myles Downey writes:

> When I am coaching, whether it is a demonstration in public or a conversation in a client's office, I occasionally rise above my normal proficiency to another level of skill and insight where there is greater fluency and not a little joy. In Inner Game terms I am coaching from Self Two, a mental state that can be achieved in which one performs with excellence, where all one's faculties are available and where one's sensitivity is heightened. This is pure flow. (Downey, 2003)

He goes on to add that, 'In Self Two our observation is more acute, we pick up more of the messages and respond in an uninhibited and congruent manner'.

Self Two is also characterised by enjoyment. Downey writes that, 'one of the quickest ways of getting into Self Two is through enjoyment'. He notes, however, that, 'What is interesting in this is that you cannot make yourself enjoy something...' He suggests that the way into enjoyment is through awareness – simply noticing how you are feeling and rating your level of enjoyment. As you do this, you may find that your level of enjoyment rises. As an exercise, you might like to reflect on the sessions or clients that you find enjoyable and those that you don't, and to consider which factors explain the difference.

A key to coaching from Self Two is trust. Tim Gallwey writes that:

> Perhaps the greatest benefit the Inner Game coach brings to the conversation is to trust clients more than the clients trust themselves. And having that trust in the client can be achieved only by having learned an increasingly profound trust in oneself. (Gallwey, 2000)

This issue of trust seems to me to be extremely important. To what extent do I trust the client to know, first, what is right for them and, second, to work out how to achieve this? To what extent do I trust myself to draw on my experience, intuition and care for the client to say or do what I need to say or do?

My first experience of working through conversation and relationship to help others was many years ago when I was a volunteer Samaritan. Working as a Samaritan isn't counselling and it isn't coaching – the implicit contract is that the client may put the telephone down at any time, and you don't know what happens next. One thing I learnt from this experience was to trust the client. I didn't know what was going to happen when they put the phone down. I had to trust them to do what was right for them. Sometimes a client would call back some weeks later and leave a message that things were better, which was great to learn. But, more often than not, I never got to know.

Trusting the client can be particularly problematic for a line manager using a coaching style of management. They may be working in an organisation whose culture is one of command and control or which more subtly does not demonstrate trust in individuals. The manager's performance is bound up with the performance of those who work for them. If you are a manager-coach, a key question to consider is *To what extent do you trust those who report to you?* Note that this is not a recipe for a laissez-faire approach to management, permitting people to underperform. But if, as a manager, you are genuinely coaching, you need to trust your people.

When I am coaching I also find it very helpful simply to trust the coaching process. If I find myself beginning to push for a solution, or starting to feel responsible for fixing things, or feeling under pressure to perform in some sense, I remind myself simply to trust the process, to be open to what is happening, and to wait to see what unfolds. This quietens my Self One and, I hope, enables me to coach from Self Two.

Sometimes coaching is ineffective. Even a skilful coach, operating from Self Two, may at times be unable to help a client. While it is important for the coach to reflect on these occasions and to be open to learning about their coaching, it may be that the client was not in a place where they were ready to change. Gallwey offers some words of reassurance to the coach who might be prone in these instances to let their Self One criticise their ability:

> Coaching cannot be done in a vacuum. If the learner doesn't want to learn, it doesn't make any difference if the coach is a great coach. Coaching is a dance in which the learner, not the coach, is the leader. (Gallwey, 2000)

14

Becoming an even more capable coach

Introduction

When drawing a coaching session to a close I often ask the client to summarise what they are taking from the conversation or what they are going to do following the session. As a coach whose style is predominantly non-directive, I think it is appropriate for the client rather than me to sum up. In this spirit, it seems fitting in this last chapter to invite you as the reader to reflect on what you are taking from the book and what you will do differently.

I would also like to note a few things that I am taking from my reflections while writing the book and to share a couple of unanswered questions that I need to consider further.

Some questions for you

I began the book by inviting you to take some time to do the silent coaching exercise. I hope that you have found some of the ideas in the book both interesting and, more importantly, of potential value in your work as a coach. I'd like to end by encouraging you to spend some time reflecting on what you have read and summarising what you will try out in practice. Here is a final set of questions for you to consider:

- What are the key insights you are taking from the book?
- What unanswered questions do you have about your coaching practice?
- What will you do differently in your work as a coach?
- When and how will you review your progress?

Some things I am taking from writing the book

The key insight that I am taking from my reflections while writing the book is an even deeper understanding that coaching is first and foremost a relationship. It is vital to create a space where the client feels safe and valued – a place from which they can begin to explore what they are seeking. There are two fundamental things that I, as a coach, can do to encourage this. The first is to listen with empathy to the client, appreciating their world and giving them really good attention. The second is to accept them unconditionally and non-judgmentally, seeing them as a unique and valuable human being. In saying this, I am reaffirming Carl Rogers' conditions for creating an effective relationship that lets the other person grow.

One of the participants on the University of Warwick Certificate in Coaching told me that I was good at 'helping folk to think', and that this can be life-changing. Helping folk to think – in ways that might sometimes be life-changing – strikes me as a worthwhile way of spending time. Coaching is about helping people to think – and, of course, sometimes to act.

Some questions for me

I am also left with some unanswered questions about my coaching. In Chapter 6, on directive and non-directive coaching, I suggested that we might modify the equation:

Awareness + Responsibility = Performance

to read:

Awareness + Responsibility + Confidence + Ability = Performance

I noted there that a development intervention might be required to help the client to develop skills and abilities. I also wrote that the coaching assignment may have to address deep-seated questions of self-confidence. This latter point – the development of confidence and self-belief – strikes me as extremely important. It poses a vital question that I need to consider – what might I as a coach do to help the client who lacks the confidence to act? I don't really have a satisfactory answer to the question, and it offers an important theme that I need to explore further.

The other set of questions that I'm mulling over at the end of the book relates to the theme we've been exploring throughout the book. Under what circumstances will I choose to be directive? And, when I choose to be directive, what will I say or do? In writing Chapter 11, on the psychological bases of coaching, I realised that I work more at a cognitive level than I had appreciated, and that by introducing particular models or frameworks I may not be as non-directive as I had thought. Writing the book has reinforced my belief in the power of being non-directive and, at the same time, has helped me to appreciate that there may be times when being directive is powerful and beneficial. I am now even more aware of the times in a coaching session when I move towards the directive end of the spectrum. And I am still reluctant to go there.

Learning to coach well is a journey without an end point. However experienced and capable a coach is, they can always be better. I wish you success, learning and enjoyment on the next stages of your coaching journey.

Bibliography

Ali, L. and Graham, B. (1996) *The Counselling Approach to Careers Guidance*, London: Routledge.

Blanchard, K. (1998) 'Servant-leadership revisited', in L. Spears (ed.) *Insights on Leadership*, New York: John Wiley., pp. 21–8.

Bresser, F. and Wilson, C. (2006) 'What is coaching?', in J. Passmore (ed.) *Excellence in Coaching*, London: Kogan Page, pp. 9–25.

Brooks, B. (2001) 'Ethics and standards in coaching', in L. West and M. Milan (eds) *The Reflecting Glass*, Basingstoke: Palgrave, pp. 95–101.

Carr, R. (2008) 'How coaches can give advice', *Personal Success*, January.

Clutterbuck, D. and Megginson, D. (2005) *Making Coaching Work*, London: Chartered Institute of Personnel and Development.

Covey, S. (1989) *The 7 Habits of Highly Effective People*, London: Simon & Schuster.

Covey, S. (1998) 'Foreword: servant-leadership from the inside out', in L. Spears (ed.) *Insights on Leadership*, New York: John Wiley, pp. xi–xviii.

De Jong, A. (2006) 'Coaching ethics: integrity in the moment of choice' in J. Passmore (ed.) *Excellence in Coaching*, London: Kogan Page, pp. 191–202.

Downey, M. (2001) 'Training for development coaches', in L. West and M. Milan (eds) *The Reflecting Glass*, Basingstoke: Palgrave, pp. 102–11.

Downey, M. (2003) *Effective Coaching*, London: Texere.

Downey, M. (2007) 'The inner game', *The School of Coaching Alumni Newsletter*, February.

Dunbar, A. (2006) 'Using metaphors with coaching', available at: *http://www.cleanlanguage.co.uk/articles/ articles/91/1/Using-Metaphors-with-Coaching/Page1 .html* (accessed 13 September 2008).

Egan, G. (2007) *The Skilled Helper,* Belmont, MA: Thomson.

Gallwey, T. (1975) *The Inner Game of Tennis*, London. Jonathan Cape.

Gallwey, T. (2000) *The Inner Game of Work*, New York: Random House.

Greenleaf, R. (1970) 'Servant-leadership', in L. Spears (ed.) *Insights on Leadership*, New York: John Wiley, pp. 15–20.

Hardingham, A. (2004) *The Coach's Coach*, London: Chartered Institute of Personnel and Development.

Harris, T. (1974) *I'm OK – You're OK*, Boston, MA: G. K. Hall.

Hawkins, P. (2006) 'Coaching supervision', in J. Passmore (ed.) *Excellence in Coaching*, London: Kogan Page, pp. 203–16.

Hawkins, P. and Smith, N. (2006) *Coaching, Mentoring and Organizational Consultancy*, Maidenhead: Open University Press.

Hobson, R. (1985) *Forms of Feeling: The Heart of Psychotherapy*, London: Tavistock Publications.

Isaacs, W. (1999) *Dialogue and the Art of Thinking Together*, New York: Currency Doubleday.

Kirschenbaum, H. and Henderson, V. (eds) (1989) *The Carl Rogers Reader*, Boston, MA: Houghton Mifflin.

Kline, N. (1999) *Time to Think*, London: Ward Lock.

Kolb, D. (1984) *Experiential Learning*, Englewood Cliffs, NJ: Prentice-Hall.

Lakoff, G. and Johnson, M. (1980) *Metaphors We Live By*, Chicago, IL: University of Chicago Press.

Lawley, J. and Tompkins, P. (2000) *Metaphors in Mind*, London: The Developing Company Press.

Lawley, J. and Tompkins, P. (2001) 'Metaphors in mind: A case study', available at: *http://www.cleanlanguage.co.uk/lozenge.html* (accessed 13 September 2008).

Margison, F. (1999) 'Robert Hobson', available at: *http://www.guardian.co.uk/news/1999/nov/29/guardianobituaries2* (accessed 13 September 2008).

Marquardt, M. and Loan, P. (2006) *The Manager as Mentor*, Westport, CT: Praegar.

Matile, L. (2007) 'Should coaches give advice?', *Personal Success*, July.

Morgan, G. (1996) *Images of Organization*, Thousand Oaks, CA: Sage.

Myers, I. (2000) *Introduction to Type* (6th edn, English European Version), Oxford: OPP.

Passmore, J. (ed.) (2006) *Excellence in Coaching*, London: Kogan Page.

Rogers, C. (1961) *On Becoming a Person*, Boston, MA: Houghton Mifflin.

Rogers, C. (1989a [1942]) 'The directive versus the nondirective approach', in H. Kirschenbaum and V. Henderson (eds) *The Carl Rogers Reader*, Boston, MA: Houghton Mifflin, pp. 77–85.

Rogers, C. (1989b [1986]) 'A client-centered/person-centered approach to therapy', in H. Kirschenbaum and V. Henderson (eds) *The Carl Rogers Reader*, Boston, MA: Houghton Mifflin, pp. 135–52.

Schwenk, G. (2007) 'Bath Consultancy Group develop four key areas of an effective coaching strategy', *The HR Director*, June.

Scott, S. (2002) *Fierce Conversations*, London: Piatkus.

Shaw, P. (2005) *Conversation Matters*, London: Continuum.

Shaw, P. and Linnecar, R. (2007) *Business Coaching*, Chichester: Capstone.

Spears, L. (ed.) (1998) *Insights on Leadership*, New York: John Wiley.

Stewart, I. (2000) *Transactional Analysis Counselling in Action*, London: Sage.

Tompkins, P. and Lawley, J. (1997) 'Less is more ... the art of clean language', available at: *http://www.cleanlanguage.co.uk/articles/articles/109/1/Less-Is-More-The-Art-of-Clean-Language/Page1.html* (accessed 13 September 2008).

Thomson, B. (2006) *Growing People*, Oxford: Chandos Publishing.

Webber, C. (2005a) 'Behaviour therapy', available at: *http://www.netdoctor.co.uk/diseases/depression/behaviourtherapy_000465.htm* (accessed 13 September 2008).

Webber, C. (2005b) 'Psychodynamic therapy', available at: *http://www.netdoctor.co.uk/diseases/depression/psychodynamictherapy_000433.htm* (accessed 13 September 2008).

Webber, C. (2006) 'Psychotherapy', available at: *http://www.netdoctor.co.uk/diseases/depression/psychotherapy_000429.htm* (accessed 13 September 2008).

Webber, C. (2007a) 'Cognitive therapy', available at: *http://www.netdoctor.co.uk/diseases/depression/cognitivetherapy_000439.htm* (accessed 13 September 2008).

Webber, C. (2007b) 'Coaching', available at: *http://www.netdoctor.co.uk/diseases/depression/coaching_000511.htm* (accessed 13 September 2008).

West, L. and Milan, M. (eds) (2001) *The Reflecting Glass*, Basingstoke: Palgrave.

Wheatley, M. (2002a) *Turning to One Another*, San Francisco, CA: Berrett-Koehler.

Wheatley, M. (2002b) 'The servant-leader: from hero to host. An interview with Margaret Wheatley', available at: *http://www.margaretwheatley.com/articles/herotohost.html* (accessed 13 September 2008).

Whitmore, J. (2002) *Coaching for Performance*, London: Nicholas Brealey.

Whitmore, J. and Einzig, H. (2006) 'Transpersonal coaching', in J. Passmore (ed.) *Excellence in Coaching*, London: Kogan Page, pp. 119–34.

Whitney, G. (2001) 'Evaluating development coaching', in L. West and M. Milan (eds) *The Reflecting Glass*, Basingstoke: Palgrave, pp. 85–94.

Whitworth, L., Kimsey-House, H. and Sandahl, P. (1998) *Co-Active Coaching*, Palo-Alto, CA: Davies-Black.

Wilson, C. (2004) 'Metaphor & symbolic modelling for coaches', available at: *http://www.cleanlanguage.co.uk/articles/articles/89/1/Metaphor--Symbolic-Modelling-For-Coaches/Page1.html* (accessed 13 September 2008).

Index

360-degree feedback, 104–7

adult:adult behaviour, 70–1, 116
– *see also* ego-states
advice, 4, 9–10, 69–75
Alexander, Graham, 5
Ali, Lynda, 75–6, 79
AM Azure Consulting, 105
Assagioli, Robert, 144
Association for Coaching, 92–3
awareness, 1, 15–16, 20–1, 31,
    54, 79–80, 110, 118, 141,
    145, 148, 158–9, 170, 175

Bath Consultancy Group, 163
Berne, Eric, 139, 142
Blanchard, Kenneth, 122
Bluckert, Peter, 62
Bonhoeffer, Dietrich, 18–19
boundaries, managing, 84–6,
    127
Bresser, Frank, 47–8
Briggs, Katharine
– *see* Myers, Isabel
British Gas, 64
Brooks, Beverly, 85, 89, 94

card sorts, 98–100
Carr, Rey, 74–5
Change Partnership, The – *see*
    Praesta

Chartered Institute of Personnel
    Development, 63
clean language, 42, 47, 129–35
Clutterbuck, David, 68
coaching:
    as relationship, 7–8, 20, 28, 42,
        59–60, 84, 109–10, 114,
        118, 174
    coaching a team, 118–19
    coaching and mentoring,
        13–15, 78–9
    coaching as a line manager,
        109–23, 171
    coaching culture, 119–20
    coaching dance, the, 76, 112–14
    coaching learning cycle, 65–6
    coaching qualifications, 64–5
    coaching trios, 55–7, 63
    defining coaching, 6–8, 78,
        138–9, 160, 164, 174
    inner game of coaching, 33,
        160–71
    silent coaching, 1–6, 21
    tools you might use in
        coaching, 95–107
    types of coaching, 11–12
Coaching Academy, 73
cognitive-behavioural approach,
    104, 137–49, 175
community of selves, 146–8
confidentiality, 84–5

congruence, 153–4
contracting, 86–90, 166–7
counselling, 13, 43–4, 75, 80–2
countertransference, 167
Covey, Stephen, 24, 121
CPS, 13–14
Crookes, Shirley, 20

Data Protection Act, 93
DBM, 88–9
de Jong, Allard, 83, 87
deference threshold, 168
directive and non-directive
    coaching, 8–13, 43–4, 67–82,
    152–3, 175–6
  dimensions of directive and
    non-directive coaching, 68
  questioning and being non-
    directive, 43–4
  some evidence, 80–2
Downey, Myles, 7, 12, 19, 28, 33,
    35, 42, 46, 64, 71, 135, 139,
    155–6, 160, 164, 167, 169–70
drivers, 143
Dunbar, Angela, 133

Egan, Gerard, 32, 34, 49–50,
    72–3, 76, 79
ego-states, 70, 140–2, 165
Einstein, Albert, 90
Einzig, Hetty, 145
empathy, 19–20, 42, 49–50, 72,
    76, 109, 153–4, 174
empty chair exercise, 101–2
ethical issues, 83–94
  codes of ethics, 83–6
European Mentoring & Coaching
    Council (EMCC), 83–4, 88
evaluation, 90–1

feedback, 60–1, 69, 71, 90–1,
    113
  – see also 360-degree feedback
Freud, Sigmund, 138, 144

Gallwey, Tim, 53, 139, 151,
    154–61, 164, 170–1
Gandhi, Mahatma, 122
Graham, Barbara – see Ali, Lynda
Greenleaf, Robert, 121
Grove, David, 129
GROW model, 5–7, 16, 32–3, 37,
    48, 54, 57–9, 72, 110, 118
  TO GROW model, 57–8
Growing People, 6, 28, 53–4,
    110–11, 117–18, 126

Hardingham, Alison, 20–1, 26–8,
    31, 33, 37–8, 107
Harris, Thomas, 141
Hawkins, Peter, 63, 118–20, 163,
    168
Hemery, David, 76, 112–14
Henderson, Valerie – see
    Kirschenbaum, Howard
Hobson, Robert, 127, 137,
    146–9
humanistic psychology, 137–49,
    159
  – see also person-centred
    approach

infantilisation, 165
information giving, 75–6
inner game, 154–8, 160
  inner game of coaching, 33,
    160–71
interference, 110, 156–9, 161–8
Isaacs, Bill, 25

Johnson, Mark – *see* Lakoff,
    George
journalling, 61–2
Joyce, Catherine, 40
Jung, Carl, 102

Kimsey-House, Henry – *see*
    Whitworth, Laura
King, Martin Luther, 122
Kipling, Rudyard, 33
Kirschenbaum, Howard, 81
Kline, Nancy, 21–2, 27–9, 40–2,
    47, 128, 164–6
Kolb, David, 54

Lakoff, George, 126
Lancaster, University of, 64,
    153–4
Lawley, James, 47, 129–35
learning cycle, 54, 65–6
learning from experience, 53–4,
    63
letter writing, 100–1
life-script, 142–3
Lifeskills Associates, 99
Linnecar, Robin – *see* Shaw,
    Peter
listening, 8–10, 17–29, 31–2, 54,
    109, 118, 123, 165
  active listening, 26–8
  levels of listening, 18–22
  listening and questioning,
    21–3
  listening for the feet, 24
  listening with the head, the
    heart and the gut, 22–4
Loan, Peter – *see* Marquardt,
    Michael

managers:
  advice and solutions from a line
    manager, 76–7
  coaching as a line manager,
    109–23, 171
Mandela, Nelson, 122
Margison, Frank, 149
Marquardt, Michael, 122–3
Matile, Lesley, 73
McGill, Madeline, 61
Megginson, David – *see*
    Clutterbuck, David
mentoring, 13–15, 78–9, 122–3
  definition, 15, 78
metaphor, 19, 22–4, 125–35, 147
Meyler, Jane, 64
Milan, Mike – *see* West, Lucy
Mitton, Michael, 26
Morgan, Gareth, 126–7
Mother Teresa, 122
Myers, Isabel, 102–3
Myers-Briggs Type Indicator
    (MBTI), 102–4

National Institute for Clinical
    Excellence, 139
note keeping, 91–4
note taking, 50–1, 60

OPP, 103
Oxford Group, The, 91

parapahrasing – *see* playing back
parent:child behaviour, 70–1, 165
  – *see also* ego-states
performance and development
    reviews, 114–15
Performance Consultants, 4, 15

person-centred approach, 73,
    151–3
playing back, 8–10, 17, 20, 23–4,
    42–3, 45–51, 54, 109, 118,
    123
potential, 110, 156–9, 161,
    168–70
Praesta, 13–14
psychoanalysis, 137–49
psychodynamic approach, 137–49
psychometrics, 102–4, 106–7
psychosynthesis, 144–6, 148
Psychosynthesis and Education
    Trust, 144–5

questioning, 5, 8–10, 17, 20,
    31–44, 54, 109, 118, 123,
    165, 167
  clarifying questions, 37
  clean language questions,
    130–1
  closed questions, 33–5
  crisp questions, 36, 97
  differentiating questions,
    37–8
  hypothetical questions, 38
  incisive questions, 40–2
  leading questions, 36, 39–40
  listening and questioning, 31–3
  open questions, 33–5
  performance and development
    reviews, 114–15
  probing questions, 37
  questioning and being non-
    directive, 43–4
  silent coaching questions, 2–4
  softening the question, 35

reflecting back – see playing back
reframing, 38–9

responsibility, 1, 15–16, 20–1, 31,
    54, 79–80, 110, 118, 141–2,
    145, 148, 158–9, 175
rich pictures, 95–8
Rogers, Carl, 80–2, 129, 134,
    139, 151–4, 159–60, 174

Samaritans, 170
Sandahl, Phil – see Whitworth,
    Laura
School of Coaching, 7, 9, 64, 167
Schwenk, Gil, 90
Scott, Susan, 25, 77
Self One and Self Two, 155–8,
    161, 164, 166, 168–71
servant-leadership, 120–3
Shaw, Peter, 94, 104, 106
silence, 25–6
silent coaching, 1–6, 21
Smith, Nick, 119–20, 168
Spears, Larry, 121
Stewart, Ian, 140
subpersonalities, 144–6
suggestions – see advice
summarising – see playing back
supervision, 62–4, 94, 168
symbolic modelling, 129–35

telling, 4, 10–11, 155, 160
  – see also coaching dance
transactional analysis (TA), 85,
    139–43, 148
Tompkins, Penny – see Lawley,
    James
Transco, 4, 13
trust, 33, 121–3, 152, 156, 168,
    170–1

unconditional positive regard, 14,
    153–4, 174

Warwick, University of, 84–6, 91
  Certificate in Coaching, 43, 59,
    67–8, 174
Webber, Christine, 137–9
West, Lucy, 11–12, 106–7, 137,
  148–9
Wheatley, Margaret, 20, 28, 123
Whitaker, David, 42

Whitmore, John, 4, 7, 15–16, 32,
  39, 79, 116, 139, 145, 154,
  159, 165
Whitney, Glenn, 90
Whitworth, Laura, 38–9
Wilson, Carol, 133–4
  – see also Bresser, Frank
Wodehouse, PG, 67